THE NATURE
OF THINGS

THE NATURE OF THINGS

Navigating Everyday Life with Grace

Jeffrey R. Anderson

BALBOA.
PRESS

A DIVISION OF HAY HOUSE

ISBN: 978-1-4525-4980-4 (sc)
ISBN: 978-1-4525-4979-8 (e)

Balboa Press books may be ordered through booksellers or by contacting:

Balboa Press
A Division of Hay House
1663 Liberty Drive
Bloomington, IN 47403
www.balboapress.com
1-(877) 407-4847

Because of the dynamic nature of the Internet, any web addresses or
links contained in this book may have changed since publication and
may no longer be valid. The views expressed in this work are solely those
of the author and do not necessarily reflect the views of the publisher,
and the publisher hereby disclaims any responsibility for them.

The author of this book does not dispense medical advice or prescribe the use
of any technique as a form of treatment for physical, emotional, or medical
problems without the advice of a physician, either directly or indirectly. The
intent of the author is only to offer information of a general nature to help
you in your quest for emotional and spiritual well-being. In the event you use
any of the information in this book for yourself, which is your constitutional
right, the author and the publisher assume no responsibility for your actions.

Any people depicted in stock imagery provided by Thinkstock are models,
and such images are being used for illustrative purposes only.
Certain stock imagery © Thinkstock.

Printed in the United States of America

Balboa Press rev. date: 4/18/2012

"What is the place of human beings in the harmony of the whole, and what does that tell us about how we ought to act in the world?"
Kathleen Dean Moore, *The Pine Island Paradox*

CONTENTS

INTRODUCTION

W/hy is it that some people are generally happy, while others are predominantly unhappy? How can we go about living our lives in a way that allows for a higher degree of happiness, or, from a more Buddhist perspective, at least with less struggle, and less suffering? How does life work? How can I navigate with less clunk, and more grace?

I have been asking these questions all of my life, and I started looking for answers early.

My best friend in junior high school was a preacher's kid. He had a nice family, and a church in a plain little building around the corner from my house. Theirs was a nice, close spiritual community, and though I didn't understand what their religion was specifically about, I did experience them as accepting, loving, kind people. I knew that they were on to something.

My best friend in high school was another preacher's kid, United Methodist this time, and again I had an experience of accepting, loving, kind people. I wasn't sure that I believed everything that they did, but I felt that they too were on to something essentially good, something that helped them to make sense of things, to suffer less, to be happy more. The love and acceptance that they extended to me affected me more significantly than I realized at the time. It felt good, and made a lifelong impression on me.

A pivotal moment in my inquiry came in my teens when I walked into a Buddhist temple in Los Angeles. It was a beautiful place, and though I had no real knowledge of Buddhism I did feel the sacred nature of that temple. I knew that the people who came to that place were every bit as holy and good as the people of the other religions that I had experienced. This presented a big problem. My experience of the goodness in that temple was in direct conflict with the "only one way to God" school of thought that I had been taught. Since I could not reconcile this, I fled religion.

In college my inquiry led to psychology, which I choose as my major. I excelled at it − when I showed up for class − but this line of inquiry ultimately felt incomplete. Although I appreciate the power of our minds more and more as time goes by, and subscribe to much that I learned then and since about human psychology, psychology alone was not fully satisfying. Something was missing.

After college I spent many years doing "field research". This consisted of all sorts of madcap adventures and various rabble rousing, and not a little experimentation in altered states of consciousness. If not in church or science, surely the key to happiness could be found in the world of wine, women, and song! That period gave me extensive perspective. While there were a lot of good times, I also learned a lot about being unhappy and feeling disconnected. In the end something still remained elusive, and my questions about life remained unanswered.

Somewhere in my 30's I was introduced to thinking that felt more in alignment with my own. Melody Beattie may have been the first New Thought writer that I encountered. She spoke to life and spirituality, thought and belief not in an exclusive, demanding way, but in an open, inclusive way. Gary Zukav's *Seat of the Soul* showed up in my life shortly thereafter, at a most opportune time, followed by the work of Wayne Dyer, Marianne Williamson and Deepak Chopra. My awareness of the nature of things began to widen and deepen.

As I write this, I am looking at the stack of books on my worktable that I reference regularly; authors like Ernest Holmes, Eckhart Tolle, Amit Goswami and Pema Chodron are regular fare. John Shelby Spong, Jack Kornfield, Ecknath Easwaren, Ram Dass and Miguel Ruiz, philosophers like Kathleen Dean Moore, poets like Emerson and Rumi and Hafiz and musicians like Rickie Byars-Beckwith have all contributed to my consideration of things. One of my Bible teachers in grad school helped me to become friends again with that amazing library of documents, and with the teachings of Jesus. I've studied the Hindu and Buddhist and Hebrew sacred texts, Taoism, Paganism, quantum physics and metaphysics. I earned a masters degree in consciousness studies along the way, and became ordained as a Religious Science minister, which is a new thought / ancient wisdom philosophy.

Through it all I found myself looking to Nature itself, at how things seem to be designed, to what is common. In my thinking, the nature of things, the nature of God if you will, must be common to all. Indigenous people seem to have known this all along. Nature is sacred and holy to them. God is not only something metaphysical, but also the physical world, the plants and animals, the mountains and rivers, the air and the sun and the earth. I like this kind of spirituality because the laws of nature do not discriminate. They are applicable whether you are black or white, male or female, Christian or Muslim or Jewish. The sun shines on all and all alike. It's not surprising that we feel good when we immerse ourselves in nature.

In our "modern" culture, we seem to have largely forgotten that the nature of Nature is our nature. The rhythms and cycles and seasons, the ebb and flow of the tides and the wandering of the river is our nature. The nature of God must be common to all of creation. Our egos may have convinced us that we are superior or somehow immune to the laws of nature, but we are not. The sooner we remember that, the happier we will be. In nature everything is connected, interwoven, subject to natural law. We cannot separate ourselves from that, no matter how hard we try.

We are all asking the same kinds of questions—students and scientists, clerks and philosophers, mechanics and theologians. We're looking at the laws of physics, the laws of metaphysics and the laws of nature, all with the same goal in mind. How do things work, and can my life be better by learning, understanding, and applying the answers that I find?

The rigid, fear-based religious laws of man are not satisfying an increasingly restless population, especially the segment recently dubbed "cultural creatives". Characteristics of this group include a love of nature and awareness of environmental and global issues, an emphasis on relationship and being in service to others, a desire for a spiritual way of life but a caution about organized religion. We're looking at how to live life in an organic, sustainable way that works for everyone, that facilitates our heart and soul desire to experience the richness and beauty, the awe and wonder, the passion and love of life that we sense is our nature to experience and to express. We're questioning things, looking for deeper meaning, seeking a gentler way of living, of walking upon the earth and through the global village. If you've read this far, you are probably a cultural creative.

We are, as a culture and as a species, in the midst of a great awakening, remembering that there is a nature of things, an inherent, Divine design. The more aware of and in alignment with that design we can become, the more we will experience the deep desires of our hearts and souls, and perhaps, together, we can truly create a world that works for everyone.

FLOW

"There is a river flowing now very fast. It is so great and swift that there are those who will be afraid. They will try to hold on to the shore. They will feel they are being torn apart and will suffer greatly. Know the river has its destination. The elders say we must let go of the shore, push off into the middle of the river, keep our eyes open and our heads above the water. And I say, see who is in there with you and celebrate."

~ Oraibi, Arizona Hopi Nation

When considering how to navigate life, I look often – and often look first – to nature. She has been doing her thing since the beginning, and doing it quite well. Left to her own devices, nature finds her way, evolves, and expands. She has her rhythms and cycles, ebbs and flows, seasons and themes that all work well individually and together as a whole.

Though nature is perhaps the best teacher to reference when considering how to navigate our own lives, we have forgotten that her nature is our nature. We have veered away from the nature of things, and as a result

1

we experience a sense of separation. When we separate ourselves in our minds from the nature of things, we lose our built-in points of reference. We get disoriented. We need to remember her secrets - that her nature is our nature - and emulate and apply that knowledge in our lives. We need to reconnect with the nature of things.

When I feel clumsy or lost, I remind myself that nature, including me, was created by a far wiser mind than mine. There is something – God, Spirit, Consciousness, Life Itself, call it what you will – in the cosmos that created and orchestrates nature, and did a good job at it. Getting all of the planets spinning just right and all spaced out so that they're not bumping into each other, breathing life into matter - things like that are no small task. Nature might just know what It's doing.

By looking to the Source, to the Creator of nature, we can remember how to navigate life organically, with less struggle and less suffering.

I remember distinctly a time that I found myself standing by a lake, in awe of the beauty of it. I was alone with the breeze, the water and the trees, and the breathtaking orchestration of life before me. Standing beside that lake, I had a realization. It was as if the lens of my perception zoomed out and I saw The Bigger Picture. I realized that I was not separate from the nature of things, was not just an observer of the beauty before me, but was included within the picture. I existed within that grand panorama. I realized that I was just as integral an ingredient in the whole of that picture as the trees and the wind and the mountains. I had a place within the Whole. I was not separate. I was viable and valuable and had purpose, even if I wasn't sure what that purpose was, because everything in the picture had purpose. In that moment of realization, I also had hope, for I realized that maybe I did belong. Maybe there was a place for me, after all.

The River ~

The river is one of my favorite metaphors, the symbol of the great flow of Life Itself. The river begins at Source, and returns to Source, unerringly. This happens every single time, without exception. We are no different.

Within the river there are long, calm stretches, much like a summer season, that find their way easily and effortless across the landscape. In these calm stretches there are deep, placid pools, the river slowly finding its way. There are shallower stretches, without the depth, but they are no less river because they are shallow. They are just shallow, that's all.

There are rapids, when the flow is turbulent, almost violent as it finds its way. Yet we don't judge its turbulence. We marvel at its power, at its ability to find its way over, around and through whatever obstacles are in its way.

There are eddies, when some part of the river seems almost trapped, going round and round upon itself, off in a corner, going nowhere. Sediment and various and assorted flotsam accumulate in these eddies, creating a stagnant appearance. Things settle in these places, and often it feels like the flow of the river has gone wrong, taken a wrong turn. But given time, and knowing that the river always finds it way, eddy's dissipate, and what was once going round and round is once again absorbed into the greater flow.

In the river one can only see as far back as the last bend, and as far ahead as the next bend. We cannot see beyond that. Nor do we need to. Ours is to navigate, as best we can, the stretch of river that we currently occupy. It is the only thing that we can do, the only thing that we need to do. We cannot go back, and what is ahead will present itself soon enough, in good time.

What we can do is be present. There is, truly, nothing else. We cannot go back and change anything. Behind us is not the same river that we navigated. The current has carried us beyond the last stretch, and it serves no real purpose for us to ruminate again and again about how we would have done it differently had we known what we do now. We did the best that we could, knowing what we knew at the time. We came through the other side, into this new, present stretch of river. We have another chance to navigate, perhaps in a slightly different way than we did yesterday. We cannot go back. But we can learn.

Nor can we go forward, around the next bend, into tomorrow, or next week, or next year. That is not where we are. We are where we are, and that is the only place that we can be. The river is already there, around the next bend. We can trust that, if we will. The river knows where it is going, even when we do not. We can trust the river, for it has and always will know where it is going. It is not required that we know all of the details about every stretch of the river. Indeed, were we to know, it would not be an adventure, and I wonder if there would be much point.

Perhaps M. Scott Peck puts it best, "An adventure is going into the unknown. If you know exactly where you are going, exactly how you will get there, and exactly what you will see along the way, it is not an adventure. If we know exactly where we're going, exactly how to get there, and exactly what we'll see along the way, we won't learn anything."

Ebb & Flow ~

Ocean tides go out, and they come back in. That is their nature. They ebb and flow. That same cyclical nature is our nature.

When the tide goes out, it seems that there is less water, less ocean. But we don't judge it, scorn it and say, "Bad tide! Bad ocean!". Do we? Of course not. It's just an ebb tide. It's the nature of things. The tide is out, and it will come back in again soon enough. Yet often, when we are experiencing an ebb time in our lives, in some area or another, we judge and label it as bad, or wrong.

A little short on money this month? Bad person! Bad economy! Bad something! Going through a cycle of not experiencing the kind of love or companionship that you want to experience? Not as kind or as understanding as you want to be in your heart of hearts? Bad person! That is about as silly as judging the ocean for an ebb tide. It happens. Get used to it. It will change soon enough, if we let it. A dry winter or two? We know that the rain will come, and that, in good time, things will even themselves out. A forest fire that seems to devastate the landscape? We know that here too nature knows what she's doing, that in fact some of the seeds and landscapes need the fires in order to ultimately thrive.

We trust nature to know what it is doing, but we are not nearly so kind, understanding and trusting of our own rhythms and cycles. It's ridiculous that we are so hard on ourselves! Can we not trust that the very same forces that created the rhythms and cycles of nature created our own? Of course we can. We often don't, but we can, if we remember.

Seasons ~

It's the first day of spring, and I am in awe and wonder at the irrepressibility of Life, how it reasserts its presence after the quiet pause of winter. How does it know how to do all that it does? Surely there is A Knowing behind it all. There is a teacher, an expresser, a creator, an artist perhaps, a poet certainly that has designed and presented all of the clues that we need to navigate life with some degree of grace, and perhaps with a greater degree of happiness than we now have.

Nature doesn't struggle with itself. Certainly there is life and there is death but, even in death, if we look closely enough, we will find grace.

The seasons are great teachers, and we can compare and contrast the seasons of our lives with the naturally occurring seasons of nature. They don't always coincide, but we can always find a parallel.

Spring ~

We all go through seasons in our lives. Winter, spring, summer and fall all occur at regular and sometimes not so regular intervals.

Spring brings with it all of the color and suppleness of re-emerging life. We are born into spring, supple and infused with seemingly limitless possibility. Clean and fresh and new, we emerge into the world bright with color, flushed with the vitality of life itself. Anything is possible in the spring of our lives, because we don't know any different! All that we have experienced is spring! We have accumulated none of the stories, none of the limiting beliefs, none of the accumulated wounds that accompany the other seasons. Life is good, and the world is full of promise.

In spring, possibility is poised at every turn. We engage life with a fearless, almost reckless abandon. There is a zest to our navigation of life. We are immortal, and life is irrepressible. Anything is possible, because we haven't accumulated any evidence to the contrary!

Clearly spring is our early lives, the time of youth and enthusiasm and vitality that seems to slosh all over with wild abandon onto everything that we do and think and say and feel.

Yet spring is not limited to the young. Spring seasons also happen frequently throughout our lives. They may or may not align with the seasons of the planet, but regardless of where on the calendar they fall, they have a very similar feel to the spring of the year, of young life; fraught with promise, brimming with vitality, curious and even reckless with an impulsion to live as big as we can.

Love is often equated with spring. If you know love, you know the feelings that it elicits. There can be ten feet of snow outside, but love can make it feel like a spring day.

Creativity can also elicit a spring experience. Indulging in passionate expression facilitates the expanded flow of that same kind of energy within us. Life energy – the Chinese would call it Chi, the east Indians, Praná – flows in vast quantities, and possibility feels truly infinite.

Whenever spring shows up in our lives, it is to be recognized, honored and surrendered to. Imagine the flowers refusing to bud and to bloom because they were having a bad day, or were worried about what the next season might bring. It doesn't happen! The birds don't wake up in the morning neurotic, worried about whether there will be enough bugs or seeds for them to eat. They don't make appointments with the bird psychiatrist for therapy or to medicate themselves so that they can cope with the fact that there are other birds with bigger nests or brighter plumage. They leap into spring, and live it to the fullest of their ability! There are things to be done! Birds live knowing that their needs will be met, and they are!

In Spring there is an implicit trust in The Orchestrator that requires little thought, elicits no fear, bares no hesitation. Life Itself jumps at the chance to express Itself in all of the magnificent ways that it does in spring, for that is its nature. And its nature is our nature. We are no different, not at all separate from the whole of things.

When spring knocks at your door, regardless of the time of year or the season of our lives, run, do not walk to that door, throw it open with wild abandon, and say "Yes! Yes, come in! Do me, and do me big!"

You would think that this is a normal and natural response, to say yes to something so delightful. Spring should be a welcome guest, whatever the package that it comes in. But I have seen, time and time again, spring left standing at the door, refusing to be acknowledged, refusing to be invited in and accepted. Why would we do such a thing?

The reasons that we leave spring standing at the doorstep are simply not good enough reasons. They are all fear-based, and often stem from a fear of loss. We have been hurt before, so why even try? I'm not creative, so why even try? It never works out for me, so why even try? I'm lousy at love, so why even try? So we leave spring standing on the doorstep, until eventually it concedes to our refusal to welcome it, and goes away.

I know we have been hurt. I know we have suffered loss. I know that we have accumulated a pile of evidence to reinforce the debilitating belief that we aren't good enough. I know. I've had to sort through my own accumulation of that evidence. I also know that life is here to be lived, and that as long as there is breath in our bodies and a heartbeat in our chest, it is our opportunity, our birthright, indeed our responsibility to live it.

There is something more important than fear. There is life to be lived. There are endless springs to be embraced. There is simply no reason good enough, no excuse strong enough, no evidence compelling enough to say "no".

When spring knocks at your door, for God's sake answer, and say, "yes, yes, a thousand times yes!"

Summer ~

Summer brings with it the halcyon days, those days in our 30's and 40's and into our 50's when life is good, the bounty of spring growth is at hand, and life can be relished and enjoyed. This is the season of families, of adventures and wanderings of a different sort than spring. It is a season of maturing perspective and accumulating wisdom. The pace of summer may be slower than spring, but it is no less full, no less fraught with the promise of abundance and warmth and life living itself fully.

Some are blessed with summers that seem to last well into what "should" be fall. This is indeed a glorious time, for we are aware of being treated to something special, a bonus from Life Itself. This is a time of grace, a time of soaking up every last moment of fullness that we know will pass soon enough.

Summer seasons show up in our lives as plateau periods, times of relative stability allowing for relaxation, of being, in good balance with doing. Summer seasons can feel like in-between times; in-between major life changes, in-between major choices and decisions, in-between the trauma and drama that seems so prevalent on our world.

Why would we mess with summer? Yet sometimes we do. We get a little restless, a little bored, or think we should be Doing more than Being. We move so fast in our culture and have agreed that moving fast is the best way to be. Sometimes that agreement can make it hard for us to sit still and, as a result, we can be so busy doing that we miss summer altogether.

Summer, like the rest of the seasons, is to be relished. Summer doesn't last forever! Allowing ourselves a summer season now and then, remembering that nature did a pretty good job designing the seasons, and knowing that it won't last forever can make it all the more sweet. Enjoy your summers, for we get a limited number of them in this lifetime.

Fall ~

Fall is a time of gratitude, a time when things begin to slow and to speed up at the same time. Metabolism begins to slow, but the pace of life seems to pick up as we realize that there is a limited time before our winter and there are things to be done before the quiet of winter begins.

I was rather startled to discover for myself that I am in a fascinating place of summer, fall and also of spring, simultaneously. Stepping into a new career mid-life seems to have facilitated this experience, one that seems to be a more and more common event in our society these days. The seasons can be very sneaky sometimes.

None the less, spring is also before me, with its endless possibility and directions to consider and court. Summer is here, for I have finally reached a point where I am not running around like a crazy person trying to do everything for everyone all of the time. I am learning how to relax and enjoy life.

Perhaps the most sobering realization is that I also sense fall in the wind. I must, at some level, have known that this was coming but honestly I find myself occasionally disoriented by the realization that I am no longer young.

My yoga teacher, some years ago, instructed the class to rest our heads on the floor, at the hairline. I was not happy to realize that her hairline and mine were in very different places. Doing inverted yoga poses is also a lovely reminder that I am no longer immune to gravity. My body doesn't stay in place like it used to.

I found myself, just recently, telling someone a "When I was a kid…" story, and was horrified. And I'm not sure that I understand the music these days.

Friends my own age are dying, and our parents are now at an age where care and end of life issues become real. This is all a rather sobering experience for us. We are not the type of people who are old. We don't do old. I for one am a kid in my heart and soul, with a love of play and adventure and short pants and Birkenstocks and the energy of youth itself. Aches and pains and physiological care and maintenance feel very foreign to me. But not as foreign as they once were.

I, for one, am praying for the longest Indian Summer in the history of the planet.

Winter ~

Winter is a time of rest, of introspection, a slowing of mind and heart and body and soul. And yes, winter is often a time of death, the great cycle complete. Life itself seems to slow in winter, to rest itself, gathering strength for another spring, in this or another place.

It may not seem like a lot is accomplished in winter. It takes understanding and wisdom to remember that everything has its place, and its time. One of my favorite passages from the Bible is in the book of Ecclesiastes. "To everything there is a season, and a time to every purpose under Heaven." This helps me to remember that everything has its place.

The seasons all have their place within the perfect whole of life. It is ours to recognize them, to align with them, and to honor them all.

CYCLES & THEMES, ORBITS & SHOEBOXES

"There are seasons and cycles in our lives, just as there are seasons and cycles to nature, to all of life. We move imperceptibly from one to the other, learning, growing, laughing and crying along the way."

~ Melody Beattie

Everything in creation moves in some kind of rhythm or cycle. Like the moon and the sun, aspects of our lives cycle periodically. If we are aware of what the rhythms and cycles are, then perhaps we will not be so surprised or even shocked when things do cycle around, presenting themselves again for our consideration. We don't need to be surprised when we are facing, one more time, something that we thought that we were done with, once and for all.

Believing that we should be done with life issues and challenges once and for all is like believing that we can eat once and for all. It doesn't work that way. Everything in life moves in rhythms and cycles. The sooner we remember that, the less we will suffer.

The rhythms and cycles of life involve themes. The realization that we have themes in our lives is important. We all have common themes, like the seasons, but we also seem to have more individualized life themes. Once we begin to identify our themes, we can consider them in a conscious, proactive way rather than in an unconscious, reactive way.

One of my teachers, a theoretical quantum physicist from India, introduced me to life themes in a very different context than I had previously considered. He proposed that what we think of in the West as the individual soul is a body of themes. This soul-body transmigrates from lifetime to lifetime, and as it does, it accumulates certain themes that are ours, as individuals in this lifetime, to consider, to shift, to re-contextualize or perhaps to heal.

This theory would explain why many of us do seem to have prevalent themes in our lives. These themes can show up as issues around relationships, money, fear, abandonment, physical health, codependence, or addictions, to name a few. Whatever our themes are, we get the opportunity to work on them throughout our lives. They show up cyclically, often in slightly different packages or circumstances than the last time, but always oddly familiar. They *are* familiar. They are a life theme for us, something that is ours to realign, to understand, ultimately to heal.

If we are awake and doing our work, we sometimes recognize these themes in our lives. Sometimes we even think we have them figured out, that we're done with them, only to have them resurface in a different way, in the form of a different person or situation. We are shocked every time a theme reappears. We shouldn't be.

When a theme cycles around in our lives, it is an opportunity to heal some aspect of it, to understand it with more depth. It may seem that we just go around in circles with some of our life themes, but in truth it is not a flat circle like a racetrack, but rather an upward spiral. When one of our themes cycles around, we are never at the same place on our life path that we were the last time it appeared – yesterday, last week, or last year. We know more, have experienced more, have accumulated more tools and wisdom, and as a result are able to view the person or situation that represents our theme from a different perspective than we had before.

Once we become conscious of the theme and the cyclical nature of it, we realize that it presents itself not because we are haunted or doomed by something that won't go away. Instead, if we are aware and willing to reconsider it with each cycle, we can gradually heal an aspect of it. With healing, it can incrementally shift, begin to dissipate, and lose some of its gravitational pull, its impact, if you will, on our lives. It may continue to orbit around periodically, but with each orbit, it has less mass. With enough consideration and healing, these orbiting themes can change from something that has wreaked havoc in our lives into simply something that reminds us of how far we have come.

Whether you subscribe to the theory that themes are something that we come into this life with, or instead that they are the result of traumatic experience early in life, we do seem to go through a season of collecting evidence that our theme exists. Over and over again we will fall into the same hole, and wonder how we got there. We may not be aware of our themes yet, and so can claim ignorance. We can accumulate a lot of pain around our themes. We may build a belief that we are somehow defective or incapable in that area of our life. We're not. It's just a theme.

We are not at the mercy of our mental or cellular memory of when the theme first appeared and caused us pain, nor are we at the mercy of the pain that we have accumulated along the way. We can, slowly but surely, piece by piece, let go of and heal our dominant life themes.

Until we become aware of them, themes are like railroad cars of baggage that we accumulate, hook ourselves up to and haul around with us on a daily basis. Most of the time we do this unconsciously. We don't even know we're doing it. Our themes and our baggage have become such a normal part of our day-to-day experience that we don't even notice the weight. And we wonder why we often feel exhausted and depleted.

By becoming awake and aware of the themes in our lives, we can begin to unpack those freight train car loads of baggage. Our load becomes lighter, more space is created in our minds and hearts, in our consciousness and in our being, and new, fresh possibility begins to pour itself into and through every aspect of our lives. We can lighten our own load.

Inventory your train cars. Find out what's in there, where it came from, and start unpacking. Start at the first day of your life and list all of the significant people in your life. Write down next to that list of names what you took away from each relationship – beliefs, fears, wounds, gifts. Become aware of where you accumulated what you have accumulated. Then you can ask yourself; is this mine? Is it true? Was it ever true? Is it true for me now?

Don't take forever to do this inventory. I realize that you may have had some traumatic event when you were six that has adversely affected the way that you experience your life, and it can be a good thing to be aware of that, and how it affects your life today. I don't want to deny anything. But don't invest huge amounts of time and energy on the telling and retelling of the story. The story keeps us tangled in our own mire more than almost anything else. And we're the only one who can stop telling it. It's time to create a new story, or at least modify the old one so that it no longer defines or confines who and what you are today. We all have a story. We all have a pathology. But if we don't change the story that we are telling ourselves, and anyone else who will listen, then nothing is going to change. That story will rise in our consciousness every morning like the sun rising in the east, and the outcome will be just as predictable.

I have a great story. In fact, I will match you story for story. We do that. We have story competitions. My story is better, more dramatic, or traumatic, than yours. It's kind of sick, but we do it.

I am not denying our life experience. I am a firm believer that everything happens for a reason, and that we are capable of turning every single thing that we have ever experienced to our advantage. But to do so, we have to break the cycle of ignorance and victimization, change the orbit, and interrupt the habit of telling and retelling the same limiting story.

These train cars that contain our story, our pathology, are like planets, moons and asteroids, orbiting around in our own little mental solar systems. They are various shapes and sizes, each with its own unique orbit, each having a different gravitational pull on our being. Some are huge, in close orbit, and influence most everything that we think, say, feel and do. Others are in a more distant orbit, elliptical perhaps, and show up cyclically, but all in our mental solar system.

The key point here is that in a solar system, it is the nature of things to orbit. It's not odd or strange that things show up either regularly or irregularly. It's the nature of things. What a relief! There is nothing wrong when issues or challenges or themes reappear in our lives. It's the nature of things to orbit!

As fully loaded train cars, they can and do have a dramatic effect on us, on our individual tides, if you will. They pull us all over the map, and if we are unaware of them in the first place we get pulled all over the mental and emotional landscape with no real clue as to why. It surprises and frustrates us every time it happens. We are essentially at the mercy of these influential mental-stellar bodies orbiting through our consciousness.

Imagine being surprised every time the moon becomes full and, as a result, the tides are extreme. We have to remember that the nature of nature is our nature. Things orbit. It's OK! It doesn't mean anything has gone wrong, or that we have made no progress towards wellness. It's just an orbit. Every time something orbits into our awareness and our experience, we are in a different place than we have ever been, and have a unique opportunity to reconsider, and reconfigure whatever theme-issue is presenting itself. With every orbit we can unpack, reconsider, release, heal or realign some portion of whatever the issue is. We may well repack it and send it back into orbit. That seems to be the way that we do things. But each time, as we unpack and let a percentage fall away, the gravitational pull becomes less. Themes may continue to orbit, and it may feel like they are exactly the same as the last time they orbited through our awareness, but they're not. They're smaller, and therefore exert less influence on our life.

Once we have made the choice, the conscious and intentional decision to start unpacking our stories, they are not the same every time they orbit through our awareness. Little bits and pieces of them fall away with every orbit, with every consideration, with every unpacking and repacking. If we choose, and navigate them mindfully and well, we can lighten them with each and every orbit. We choose to be conscious and intentionally aware of these influences on our lives. We are in a very different place each time we experience these orbits. Life is an upward spiral path, one that moves us to higher and higher levels of awareness, of choice, and, as a result, of freedom. It may feel very much like, "oh here is THIS THING again!", and yes, here it is again, but it is not the same as last time. It has less weight, less mass, and therefore less gravitation pull on our being.

One day we realize that these orbiting masses are no longer train cars, they are pick-up trucks! Oh joyful day! They are still the same color, and flavor, and have a very similar feel, but weigh MUCH less, and as a result have much less impact on our lives!

This theme awareness and unpacking doesn't happen overnight. We get to the place where that freight car can then be loaded into a semi-trailer. This may not seem like a big improvement but, trust me, rubber tires move much easier than steel on steel. A progression happens to smaller and smaller trucks, then to moving boxes, and finally, with time and willingness, to shoeboxes. I can live with shoeboxes.

There has been much talk in psychological and spiritual community (forever) about healing, defined as the complete removal of any and all wounds, themes, and scars that in any way inhibit the full expression and experience of life. I'd like to propose a slightly different take on this.

In my own life, in my consciousness, I have a rather small closet in the corner of my consciousness where my shoeboxes are stored. I have not been able to exorcise them fully and completely. Honestly, I wonder if we are supposed to. I wonder if those little shoeboxes that contain the remnants of the freight-train cars of accumulated baggage and themes don't still serve me somehow. They are a part of my experience, after all, and they do serve as powerful reminders of where I have been, of how far I have come, and of where I do not need to revisit.

This idea that we, with enough work and persistence, willingness and high consciousness can become immaculate might be a set up for failure.

What happens after we have healed huge wounds, have come to terms with, forgiven and shifted a huge portion of what we are here to do, only to have a theme cycle through our lives again? Unfortunately, according to our current definition and goal of being immaculate, we have failed. We may have shifted, metaphorically, tons of baggage and excess freight, created huge spaces for new possibility in our lives, even created a whole new experience of life, yet some remnant of our history files remain, and because of our rigid definition of healing and our rigid expectation of perfection, we still fall short.

In truth, we have not failed at all. We have come great distances, healed major issues, freed ourselves from perhaps lifetimes of baggage. We haven't failed. We have healed, and we remain human. That is not failure. That, in my mind, is grace.

What we need to do is to redefine healing, redefine perfection, redefine what it is that we are trying to accomplish here. Life is about direction, not destination. We cannot know our ultimate destination, so why don't we focus on direction rather than destination? I have found it be a much gentler, much more organic process.

We know in our heart of hearts when we are headed in a good and right direction. We know when our direction is in alignment with the nature of things. We know, as Whitman says, when something insults our soul, or when we are acting or choosing out of alignment with our higher good. We know these things. We can and do deny that we know, but we know. You know it, and I know it.

This does not mean that we will always, unerringly, immaculately make the highest and best choices and decisions. It doesn't mean that we will be completely free of the quirks and foibles and idiosyncrasies and even neurosis that make us unique individuals. It does not mean that, once we have an understanding of the themes in our lives and the cycles that present those themes for our consideration that we will always make perfect choices every moment in every circumstance. We are human beings, not robots, and we are far from immaculate. It might serve us well to concede that.

If the choices that we are making today are better than the choices that we made yesterday, if the direction that we are moving in is healthier than it was last week, or last year, if we are not stuck and rigid in our attachment to our story, or to how we think our transformed immaculate lives have to look in order for us to be "successful", but instead are growing and expanding our consciousness and healing our wounds, then we need to cut ourselves some slack, give ourselves credit for how far we have come, and be as grateful as we can be that we are farther along the path than we used to be.

Once in a while I do get this crazy urge to walk into that shoebox closet in my mind, pull down one of the shoeboxes, dump it on the floor and roll around in its contents for a while. Maybe it has just orbited around again, and it's time to take another look. Maybe I need to remember something, or let another little piece of it fall away. Maybe it's just the nature of things to revisit our lessons now and then, so that we don't forget what we have learned. Then, when I am done, I pack it back up in its shoe box, vacuum the floor, and wander off after something else that has gotten my attention. I close the door behind me, and let my closet be.

Immaculate is not the object of the game for me anymore. I am at peace with my shoeboxes. I can live with them. Perhaps one day those shoeboxes will fit into even smaller boxes, into an even smaller place in my consciousness. That seems to be the trend, and I am open to that possibility. I am open to the possibility of them disappearing completely. And in the meantime, my closet is manageable. I have, much of the time, achieved the level of healing and peace and wellness that I set out to experience.

What were once Sun and Saturn sized issues have lost much of their mass and have much less impact when they orbit through my awareness. The orbits themselves have gotten larger, more elliptical. My mental solar system is much less congested that it has ever been. I still have themes that I think of as having Pluto orbits. They're still there, but small, and faint, maybe not even planets anymore, and they don't orbit through my awareness too often. Occasionally, but not often.

When they do orbit into my awareness, I am no longer surprised, no longer shocked and thrown completely off-balance because, "Here THIS is again!". I recognize it for what it is, and know that I am in a much different place today than I was yesterday or last week or last year. I recognize that this orbit is different than the last, that the challenge, the issue, the theme has less mass, less weight, and has significantly less impact or influence on my life. It's not the same thing all over again. Indeed, it is very, very different.

I have become familiar with my own mental solar system. I have inventoried, unpacked, and unhooked from my train cars. I have lightened my load, made space for something new and different, and life has changed dramatically.

It's not necessary to postpone our good until we have completely eliminated even the shoeboxes that contain the remnants of our major life themes and issues. By coming to terms with them, seeing how, after all is said and done, they do have their place within the whole of life, and embracing them for the teaching tools that they are, we can experience good right now, today. There is plenty of good in the world to be experienced. We just need to make room for that good in our own lives.

It's not about being immaculate. It's not about elimination, but about inclusion, and acceptance. It's about being at peace with and recognizing the Divinity of what is. That is the healing that we are seeking. We don't have to be immaculate to experience the wellness and balance and harmony that is the nature of things.

Yes, I still have shoeboxes in that little closet in my consciousness. And I thank God almost every day that they are not the train cars that they used to be. I don't beat myself up that they still exist, but instead I rejoice in the lightness of the load.

SUPPLE VS. RIGID

"Men are born soft and supple; dead, they are stiff and hard. Plants are born tender and pliant; dead, they are brittle and dry. Thus whoever is stiff and inflexible is a disciple of death. Whoever is soft and yielding is a disciple of life. The hard and stiff will be broken. The soft and supple will prevail."
~ *Tao Te Ching*

Branches sway in the slightest breeze. Even when things appear still, there is constant movement, a bending that allows for the ever-changing conditions of the environment. Over time, if branches don't remain supple, moving and bending to accommodate the air that is constantly moving around them, they become rigid, and when the wind blows too hard or the weight becomes too heavy, they don't bend. They break.

People are designed in the same way. In mind, body, heart and soul we are designed to be supple, to move and to bend in constant movement as the environment and conditions of life change, both around us and within us.

We have a pretty good awareness of this on a physical level. We exercise our bodies, stretching our muscles and promoting the flow of blood and nutrients into our cells. This flow also carries away with it that which no longer serves our bodies. Flow is a miraculous thing that way. We are eating more mindfully, remembering that we cannot promote a high level of physical wellness with a diet consisting only of highly processed foods with a high chemical content, or foods that have been produced in ways that are out of alignment with our reawakening consciousness. We're drinking more water and tea, and less coffee and soda.

We exercise and eat well because it nourishes and cleanses and keeps vital the fabric of our physical being. But how are we keeping our mind and heart and soul healthy and vital and supple?

The Mind ~

Our minds have incredible power. We are beginning to remember, through new thought spirituality, theoretical quantum physics, ancient wisdom and many other avenues of learning and inquiry just how powerful our thought is.

Notice that I am referring to mind, and not brain. I am not a brain scientist. I have done some study about the brain and have a rudimentary understanding of the function of it, but I'll leave brain function to be explained by brain people.

Mind is different, and is explored and defined in a variety of different ways. For the purposes of this inquiry, and the idea of keeping the mind supple, I'm defining the mind as a collection of beliefs, positions, facts and information that we use to navigate our lives and our world.

We collect information from the moment we're born. We may come into this life with themes or predispositions. We accumulate experiences, which are influenced by other people's experiences. We form beliefs of our own. We borrow beliefs from those around us. Our family and culture of origin teach us their values, and what is right and wrong. The media tell us what is true, and Madison Avenue tells us what we need to buy or look like in order to be happy. We watch, and we absorb, and we assimilate. This is all accumulated, contextualized, and navigated within the individual mind. That accumulation of beliefs becomes our worldview, the way that we see and interpret the world around us.

There are also "group minds" that we all participate in. When I say group mind, I am referring to things like the male or female group mind, the eastern or western culture group mind, the Republican or Democratic or upper or middle or lower class group mind. There are literally thousands of group minds - perhaps as many as there are people - that all have beliefs, agreements, positions, and opinions. Many of the beliefs in a specific group mind are obvious and clear. Most are more subtle, and operate on a subconscious or unconscious level. We don't even know that we have agreed to them. But we have.

For example, I continue to be amazed at what I find in the western male group mind. Frankly, the 21st century western male group mind is a rather confusing place to be. All of our history tells us that we are the strong ones, the hunters, the providers; me man, you woman. 99.9% of human history has carved those beliefs deeply into our minds, placed them firmly in our consciousness.

We also find ourselves in a place where we are encouraged to embrace our feminine side, to feel and express our feelings, to ache, to be vulnerable, and to weep. Yet when we do, we have a historic guilt that is often reinforced by our rather confused society telling us that we are somehow weak or soft, not real men.

What is a 21st century man to do?

I don't want to get too far off-track into that particular subject - volumes can be written on this - but you can see how many obvious, not so obvious, and often conflicting beliefs exist within just one group mind!

This is not the only group mind that we get to consider on a daily basis. There is the northern California group mind (it's amazing how significant a role geography plays in our belief systems), the spiritual group mind (which has about a zillion sub-groups), the generational group mind, the special interest group minds (also about a zillion to choose from), and the list goes on and on. All of these group minds significantly influence the way that we see, think, and feel about our lives, our world, and the people in it. We base our worldview on this eclectic, individual accumulation of beliefs, values and position. Group mind affects our entire experience of life.

The challenge here is to be awake, to own and to take responsibility for as many of our beliefs as we are aware of, and to become more and more aware as we go along. An excellent way to stay awake and conscious of what our worldview is, and why, is to continually challenge our existing belief system. This provides us with an ongoing opportunity to check and double check whether our current beliefs – which are largely our past beliefs, or someone else's beliefs – are true for us now, are valid now, are in alignment with our heart and soul.

Scientists tell us that we think essentially the same thing today that we thought yesterday, unless and until we challenge those thoughts, and introduce new ones. This kind of repetitive thinking leads to mental calcification, a hardening of our beliefs that makes us mentally rigid. When we're rigid, we're not open to new thoughts, new perspectives, and new possibilities. We attach to our pre-existing belief systems and hold on for dear life. We often hold on to beliefs long past their expiration date.

The ego hates to admit that it doesn't have everything all figured out. We love to be right. We learned in school that there is one right answer, and if you don't have the right answer, you have a wrong answer. But what if there is more than one right answer? What if, in fact, there are a lot of right answers? Could it be? Could our belief system about there being one right answer be wrong? It absolutely could be, and indeed is wrong. We learned something that is not true. Now we get to unlearn it.

This has huge implications. Can two people both be right, even when they disagree? Can two organizations, or political parties, or countries? Can we be supple enough in mind to consider that there may be other valuable, viable positions that are different from our own? It takes a supple mind to even consider the possibility.

Study as a mental or spiritual practice enables us to consider something new, every day, and in the process, to keep our minds supple.

I have a friend, a woman in her 80's who is extremely bright, vital, and open-minded. Her mind is supple, because she studies, considers new things, reads and writes poetry and enjoys art. She studies humanity and spirituality and, as a result, has one of the most supple minds that I know.

It would have been easy for her to grow rigid in her beliefs. She has not had the easiest life path. She could easily have fallen into being a victim (another extremely powerful group mind), but she chose instead to continue to consider new thoughts, new ways of looking at things, and new perspectives that have allowed her to live a rich and fulfilling life. She is a good teacher for me.

The invitation is to challenge yourself, challenge your beliefs, challenge again and again the way that you see things. The ego may not like it, but perhaps there is more than one way of looking at the world. Perhaps there is more than one right answer.

The Heart ~

I watched a video recently of soldiers returning home from their tours of service. It was a compilation of scene after scene of totally unrestrained, uninhibited love being expressed and experienced. It was a 10 minute video, and I was in tears for most of it (despite my manly-man group mind opinion that I was being wimpy).

The heart is so much more than just an organ in the body. I've studied just enough HeartMath (http://www.heartmath.com/) to be dangerous, but what I have learned is that the heart has a mind and a power all of its own. It delights, it aches, it longs. And, it defends.

I don't know of anyone that has not experienced heartache. Perhaps the most sensitive aspect of our being, the heart is tender, and easily wounded. Often when that happens, we react in a way that shuts down or isolates our hearts. We build thick, rigid walls so that we don't have to feel pain. What we might not realize is that in the process of defending, we also wall ourselves off from everything else.

Our hearts will get hurt. We might as well concede that. Heartache is not something that is inflicted upon someone because we're bad, or wrong, or somehow defective. It happens, and it happens to everyone. And we need time to heal when we hurt. It's important that we honor that. When an animal is wounded, it crawls into the bushes or into a hole to heal.

There is a difference between a wounded animal and wounded person. A wounded animal doesn't stay under the bush or in its hole for one moment longer than it needs to. When it is sufficiently healed – not completely, 100% healed, but sufficiently healed to begin to carry on with life – it crawls back into the light, and continues living.

From a spiritual perspective, each individual heart is a place where Divine love is expressed and experienced. That's what it's designed for. That love shows up in an unlimited number of shapes and sizes, colors and flavors. We are here to love, as big and as fearlessly as we possibly can.

With that as our primary task in life, there is risk, or at least the experience of risk. There will be pain along the way when we love. There is no such thing as pain-free guarantee. But as Anias Nin constantly reminds me, "And the trouble is, if you don't risk anything, you risk even more."

When we allow the walls around our hearts to become rigid, and stay that way, we assign ourselves a slow death. Like the very air and water that flows through our physical body to sustain it, love must flow through our heart to keep it supple, and to keep us truly alive.

The Soul ~

How do we go about keeping the soul supple? And what is the soul anyway?

I was raised protestant Christian, and though the soul was mentioned occasionally, I didn't really get what it was, or what it meant to me. All that anyone seemed to know for sure about my soul was that if I didn't behave, my soul is was in serious danger of burning in hell forever. That was the extent of my early soul education.

Since then I have studied and considered many opinions and positions regarding the human soul. I have also had a number of personal experiences that have given me a much broader context about what the soul might be.

Someone once said, "We are not human beings having a spiritual experience. We are spiritual beings having a human experience." This is a good place to start when considering the human soul. The soul is, perhaps, that "spiritual being" that has been given a human body for a lifetime, and tasked with living.

I've already mentioned that one of my teachers calls the soul "the body of themes". His position is that we come into this life with themes, things to consider, awaken to, realign, or to heal.

I also like a model presented in the Upanishads - sacred Hindu texts - which states that we inhabit not one but five bodies — physical, vital, mental, soul, and bliss (the God body). I like this model. Whether or not it is true, it gives me a context, a point of reference, a starting place.

My own experience leads me to believe that we inhabit a soul body, one that is distinct from the physical body and that it is immortal, if not eternal. It is not limited by the human experience, and perhaps transcends the single human lifetime. The soul seems to inhabit a place where form mingles with the formless, where humanity mingles with divinity.

I didn't know any of this when I had my first out of body experience. Yes, I'm one of those. I know, it sounds a little far-fetched, and believe me, at that time of my life the last thing that I was considering or looking for was something like this. But there it was. It happened, and is undeniable.

These experiences happened during a particularly challenging period of my life. At that time I was bouncing along a very low bottom, on a lot of levels. I had broken my back a couple of years before, had lost everything including my health, my marriage, my home and career and status and just about everything else that I held dear. I had lost everything that I defined myself by. I was feeling about as broken as a man can feel and still survive, and reached a point where my soul said, "Enough. I'm out of here.", and began to leave my physical body behind.

It began happening at night, and at first I thought that I was just dreaming. I became more aware of what was happening as this experience continued for days and then weeks. I knew that this was something very different than a dream.

My next conclusion was that I had finally jumped the mental tracks in a big way, and was going nuts. At that point, since everything else in my life had come apart at the seams, it didn't seem unreasonable to me that my mind might be doing the same thing. But it wasn't that either.

I was just an observer at first, experiencing this phenomenon that I had not created or anticipated. As the experiences continued I became more and more curious, and rather than just be an observer, I became an active participant. I began to influence, even to choose where my soul went once it left my body. I hesitate to use the word choose, because it was not choice as we normally use the word. It was mental, but not logical.

It's difficult to describe, but when my normal points of reference fell away, my process changed. The soul does not navigate life in the same way that we normally do in our waking state, which is more ego or mentally oriented. Instead it was as if I was thinking more with my heart than with my brain. My soul followed my heart, and when my soul left my physical body behind, I often went to check on people that I loved.

I became aware that it wanted to happen, this separation of soul-body and physical body. I began to sense, in advance, when and how it would happen. Once I got used to the idea, I/we/me would actually put my physical body to bed, tuck it in and make sure all of its needs were met, and then off my soul would go.

These experiences removed any doubt, and answered absolutely the one critical point, the one deep question that remained unanswered from my childhood religious education; do we really have a soul? Now I know that the answer is yes, we do embody or inhabit some kind of conscious awareness that is distinct from the physical body. Even after all of the study that I have done since then, I still cannot define the human soul for you. I can, however, assure you that I, you, we, have one.

This realization that the human soul exists may be the first step in considering how to keep it supple. Simply acknowledge its existence. Even acknowledging the possibility of its existence might be enough. That alone allows our awareness to creep beyond what it has known, beyond what it has experienced up until now.

If we allow for the possibility of a human soul, it allows for us to sit with some very interesting questions. What might there be for us to know, to consider in that place where form mingles with the formless, where humanity mingles with divinity? Seekers and mystics have been asking these questions since the dawn of time. I don't know if we can find all of the answers from where we sit in this human experience, but I do know that there is great power in simply asking the questions.

Perhaps my old teacher was right, and it is a body of themes, things that we can recognize and consider, realign and heal. Perhaps we come into this human experience with a purpose, or many purposes. The more I observe, the more it seems that individuals *do* have purposes, some clearly evident, some much more subtle. We all know nature people, or dog people, or relationship people or anger people or victim people. We know kindness people and giving people and loving people. Simply being aware of this possibility keeps the door open to suppleness of soul.

We can take it a step further. If the awareness that we really do inhabit a soul comes, we can pay attention and, from this expanded awareness, consider what presents itself for us to consider. We do have some degree of choice in the matter. Most people choose to blow this off, to ignore it, repress it, deny it, and I understand why. If there is soul work to be done, surely it will be the most challenging work before us in this lifetime. We have little context, and few points of reference. The linear, scientific models and tools that we are using in our search for knowledge fall short when we step into the realm of the soul. It can make us feel inept, impotent, and incapable of this kind of inquiry. We have to leave the familiar points of reference behind to do soul work, and some people are just not willing to do so.

Are you willing to take a look beyond the day to day stuff, into your own heart and soul? Are you willing to sit in the questions and experience the satisfaction that comes just from that? Are you willing to ask, and just as important, are you willing to listen? Are you willing to reconsider everything that you ever thought you knew, to look at things from multiple, even conflicting perspectives? Are you willing to consider the possibility of letting your whole life shift in order to bring it into alignment with your soul, and what your soul is trying to accomplish?

These are questions that we all have to ask and answer for ourselves. In my experience this is not easy work. In my own life, my whole identity had to be stripped away in order for me to look beneath it, and there were times that I did not feel up to the task. I resisted, was rigid, not willing or able to look at this aspect of myself. My mind was not supple enough to expand and allow room for my soul.

But my soul would not be denied. In the end, my rational mind conceded that there was something much greater going on, something more than just my linear experience of life. That concession, in and of itself, changed everything.

STRUGGLE AND SUFFERING

"For it is only the finite that has wrought and suffered; the infinite lies stretched in smiling repose."

~ Ralph Waldo Emerson

Suffering is in direct proportion to struggle. The more we struggle, the more we suffer. Reciprocally, the less we struggle, the less we suffer. It's that simple.

The realization that suffering seems to be in direct proportion to struggle started to form itself some years ago as the result of one of my teachers, a beautiful old Buddhist, who used to respond to many of my questions with the same answer. "Jeffrey," he would say, "attachment is the cause of all of your suffering."

I didn't understand that answer for a long time. I figured it was one of those canned Buddhist responses that teachers use when they don't know the real answer to the question. I wanted to fire that teacher more than once, but something kept me coming back. Besides, he wouldn't have cared if I had fired him. He wasn't attached.

As time went by I realized that he was wiser than I initially gave him credit for. I thought often about this, his favorite response to my questions. "Attachment is the cause of all of your suffering." I began to realize that he just might be right.

We do get attached. Another way to think of attachment is to replace the word "attach" with the word "stuck". We get stuck in habits, patterns, conscious and unconscious ways of thinking, believing, doing and living that are not serving our highest and best good. We become attached to fears and positions that are impeding, inhibiting or holding us back from our fullest expression and experience of life.

Once we get attached to limiting beliefs and positions that are not in alignment with the nature of things, there will inevitably be struggle. And where there is struggle, there is suffering.

We know when we are out of alignment. We can feel it, physiologically, energetically, mentally, even at a soul level. We may be so attached, so identified with our positions that we dare not consider what the real source of this internal dissonance is, but we cannot, ultimately, deny that it exists. I have not yet met a single person on this planet that has not experienced internal dissonance of some kind at some point along the way. Not one.

We *think* that "they" – the people that we aspire to be, the ones that we think have it all together - are free from dissonance. This creates a conflict of its own, because it is not an accurate assessment. We set about comparing our insides with the snapshot that we take of their outsides, and come to the conclusion that "they" have it all together and we don't, therefore there is something wrong with us. This leads us to shame, to internal struggle that is irreconcilable because it is based on a false assumption, which then leads, inevitably, to suffering.

We get attached to the idea that we are somehow "less than". This is perhaps our biggest attachment, the cause of much of our struggle, resulting in great suffering.

We also get attached to the idea that any dissonance, anything that challenges us or causes discomfort, is a bad thing. It's not that we need to suffer unnecessarily, but if there was never any challenge at all, would we ever change and expand and allow for new thoughts and ideas?

This whole idea of being free from dissonance 24/7/365 as being the object of the game is seriously flawed. But if some dissonance in life is inevitable, isn't suffering inevitable too? Not necessarily. What if we reconsider our definitions? What if what we have defined as struggle is simply the nature of things, something that happens on occasion, indeed that must happen on occasion to facilitate growth and change, and is normal and natural? This point of view allows us to lean into the occasional dissonance rather than fight against it. By changing our minds, we can learn to experience what we have defined in the past as struggle without suffering. It is possible to navigate dissonance with grace.

There is an old phrase, "restless, irritable, and discontent", and whenever I find myself in that condition, or experience someone else who is, I know that they, or I, are on the verge of some kind of internal shift. This symptomology happens when something is seeking to be realigned. The restless, irritable and discontent feelings that we are having are an invitation to step back, release our attachment, and allow whatever shift, realignment or creative process that is looking to happen the space to do so.

Our suffering often comes from our unwillingness to be supple enough to let things move. We can and do spend months, years, even decades expending tremendous effort to keep things in place that are out of alignment. Meanwhile these positions or opinions or beliefs are seeking only the freedom to shift or expand. They are struggling to move. We are suffering because we refuse to allow it.

We often get attached to an idea that to allow things to change is to admit defeat, or failure. We are attached to the status quo, even if that status quo is not working so well. We get stuck in unpleasant states, and our pride and ego refuse to consider the possibility that there may be a better alignment, a better way to be. We forget that nature is never static, but is always creating and expanding. That nature is our nature.

There are times when a structure needs to come down so that something new can be built. But we, spackle knife in hand, continue far beyond the structure's natural date of demise to spackle like mad people, attempting to keep something intact and presentable even though it has outlived its usefulness. We continue hanging on, attached, suffering, sometimes even stepping into righteous martyrdom in our suffering. Our message to anyone who will listen is, "See what I'm doing? See how much I am suffering to persevere? Aren't I noble?"

I don't see the nobility in this anymore. Yes, an existing structure or dynamic may be familiar, it may be "the way it's always been", or even "the way it is supposed to be." But if the way it has always been done is causing great struggle and suffering, then clearly that is not the way it is supposed to be. Our attachment to the idea of the way it is supposed to be is the cause of our struggle. What if there is another, better idea that we just haven't thought of yet, or that we *have* thought of but simply refuse to consider because of our attachment to the old idea?

We are very stubborn. We can also be very afraid of changing what we know, what we have become familiar with, regardless of how uncomfortable the familiar may be. And so we stay, even as something else within us is saying, "no, no more". We inherently know that the Nature of the Cosmos is for us to experience and to express as much good as we can embody, as much as we are *willing* to embody. Change is the nature of things.

So how do we go about aligning ourselves – thought, word and deed – with this organic state of being that we sense in our heart of hearts is available to us? How do we remain supple in mind, and as a result, suffer less?

First, we might want to reconsider our position that the brain knows best. We think way too much. The brain is a place where all of our accumulated stuff lives. What if what we have accumulated is inaccurate? What if it's not true, or is outdated? What if there is something that we haven't experienced or thought of yet? Do we have the courage and the suppleness of mind to consider that in this Universe of infinite possibility, there may be other choices that we can make, other options, other possibilities?

Look to your heart and soul first, rather than looking to your head first, when choosing. Rather than what you think, consider instead how things feel. Look to the nature of things. *Feel* your choices and decisions. It just might change everything.

We know how to align ourselves. We were born aligned. It is our nature to be aligned. If you are suffering, look at what you are attached to. Ask your heart and soul if there might be another choice. Ask if there might be a new idea to say yes to.

WAVES

"There are two dimensions to life, and we should be able to touch both. One is like a wave, and we call it historical dimension. The other is like the water, and we call it the ultimate dimension, or nirvana. We usually touch just the wave, but when we discover how to touch the water, we receive the highest fruit that meditation can offer."

~ Thich Nhat Hanh

Life moves in waves. Light, sound, energy, thoughts, feeling, emotions, even possibility itself are all waves that crash upon the shores of human consciousness. We describe our feelings as waves; waves of anguish, waves of heartache, waves of pleasure and waves of ecstasy. Waves are the nature of creation. They are, perhaps, how the Creator does what It does, as creation.

Is The Creator Itself a wave entity? That I cannot tell you. I can tell you that there seems to be an essential nature that is not subject to the waves of creation. God seems rather unflappable that way. It is greater than It's creation, yet creation embodies the attributes of the Creator. Waves must at least be some aspect of the Creator, but not all of It.

Regardless of what the essential, transcendent nature of God is, God as creation is all about waves. The wave is the signature of every experience in life. By understanding the nature of waves and their characteristics and applying that understanding to our lives, we can navigate life with a little more grace.

Waves are fluid, always in motion, never fixed or static. They have a few essential parts; a front slope, a peak, and a backside. They have a beginning, middle, and end. Waves are energy in motion. Energy carries the wave, and is embodied within it. As a wave reaches a shore or any less movable, less fluid, or opposing mass – the wave energy crashes onto the shore, and is expended. A fluid wave meets a solid destination and the wave expends, moves through, and recedes. Waves come to pass.

An interesting thing about waves is that the very same wave, with the very same energy, will behave very differently depending on the geography of the mass or shoreline that it is approaching. The way that the wave behaves and experiences itself depends as much on the shore that it finds itself encountering as it does on the energy of the wave itself. As a wave approaches, the terrain of the approaching shoreline influences whether the wave develops into something huge or if instead it simply becomes another average, everyday wave.

This is important to consider, since it is our consciousness, our lives that we are talking about. We are the shoreline. How we choose to configure ourselves mentally, emotionally and spiritually determines how the waves of life are experienced.

Like waves in the ocean, feelings and emotions, challenges, trials and tribulations are going to happen. Waves are the nature of things, the nature of creation. Storms of various and assorted configurations and intensities are an inherent part of life, and there is no escaping them.

A rather odd agreement that many of us have made, perhaps unconsciously, is that the object of the game of life is that there be no waves, no challenges, no rocking of the boat. If we are doing everything correctly, life should just be smooth sailing all of the time.

The problem with this agreement is that it sets us up mentally, emotionally and spiritually to resist the waves. We become rigid. There is no 'give', no flex, and no suppleness when challenge does happen. The wave meets an immovable object – our resistance to the wave nature of things – which results in a collision every time. Every challenge that comes along looks and feels like a tsunami, and can do just as much damage to our mental, emotional and spiritual landscape.

This group agreement – that there be no challenges, that life should be smooth sailing all of the time – is simply not realistic. It's not even healthy. It's not in alignment with the nature of things. Change is the nature of life. Waves happen, and are going to happen whether we like it or not.

Consider the electrical waves that our hearts generate. A flat line is not a desirable state of affairs. The same scenario applies to brain waves. When those go flat, it's not a good thing. Why would we think that the other waves in our lives are any different?

There is another belief that comes into play here. This one says that change and challenge are always (or most always) a bad thing, to be avoided like the plague. What an odd agreement. Waves aren't bad. Change and challenge isn't bad. They are the nature of things. The sooner we get used to that idea, the sooner we will stop suffering unduly because of them.

What if we agreed instead that change and challenges are the nature of things, that Life Itself is always looking to uplevel our capacity to embody, experience and express, and that every single change and challenge that happens is simply Life Itself growing us and making space for more of Itself in and as us? How might that agreement change our experience of life?

The question is not whether or not change and challenge are going to happen. They are. The question is, when they do happen, how are we going to choose to look at them, contextualize them, and navigate them?

The group agreement that life should be smooth sailing 24/7 is also in direct conflict with another group agreement. This agreement says that drama is a good thing. We have fallen in love with drama, and have agreed on a group level to some deranged kind of drama competition. I have drama, therefore I am.

In soap operas, if there is no drama, there is no story, and as a result there is no interest. There are few true waves in soap operas. Instead the story-line leaps from peak to peak. Valleys are so boring.

Have you ever met someone who just loves drama, and seems very capable of manufacturing it on an ongoing basis? Challenging and even dramatic things do happen in life. We have just forgotten how to let these times and events move through our lives like waves. Rather than allowing the wave to do what it is designed to do, we get up to the peak of that baby, break out the camping gear, and pitch a tent. We tell and re-tell the story, continuing to fuel an energy that is not designed to be sustained, but rather is designed to be experienced, to move through our lives, and then to dissipate and recede.

We have become a little too attached to the 'peak' of the wave. We're peak junkies. Good or bad, we love that peak. But that "pitch a tent" mentality is not in alignment with the nature of a wave and, therefore not in alignment with the nature of energy, thoughts, feeling, and emotions. It's not the nature of things. The sooner we recognize that, accept it, and align our worldview and the way that we navigate life with it, the less we will struggle and suffer.

Waves come to pass. I must have read a thousand times in the Bible when I was a kid, "And it came to pass…". Never once in that collection of books that is the Bible does it say, "and it came to stay…". It came to pass. Waves, feeling, experiences, even our physical bodies are transient by nature.

Is there anything in life that is exempt from this wave nature? Perhaps. While waves are the vast majority of what we experience in our lives, and it serves us well to know and to remember their nature as it applies to our lives, there does seem to be that which is not affected by anything in creation. That is the changeless, timeless Presence that many people call God, the Heart and the Mind of the Cosmos. It is to that One Sure Thing, the One Eternal Presence that, in the end, after we experience the very last wave of our lives, we will return.

MINDFUL WANDERING

"Come, whoever you are! Wanderer, worshipper, lover of leaving. Come, this is not a caravan of despair. It doesn't matter if you've broken your vow a thousand times. Still and yet again, come."

~ Rumi

There are no straight lines in nature. Not one, anywhere. That is the nature of things. We seem to have agreed, however, that the most desirable and efficient path from point A to point B is a straight line. This agreement creates an obvious problem. It sets us up to be in direct contradiction with the nature of things. And we wonder why we suffer.

The river as a metaphor for life is an amazing teacher. We could learn everything that we need to know about navigating life by considering how a river navigates its path.

Never in the history of the planet has a river run in a straight line from its source to its destination. Never. It winds its way, wandering over the landscape, patiently yet persistently finding its way under, around or through anything that stands in its way. Along its course the river travels through many environments and takes many forms. It may appear to have lost its way, or even disappear underground, yet as long as it remains a river it continues to flow, and along every inch of its path it nourishes everything that it comes into contact with. In return, it is kept vital by all that it experiences.

A snapshot of the river in one place cannot fully capture the essential nature of the whole of the river. A river may be many things, but is never fixed or static. It is always flowing, always changing. The Greek philosopher Heraclitus stated a long time ago, "You can never step into the same river twice."

The river may be wide and smooth, slow and placid and calm. Its path may narrow, thundering through gorges, or become shallow rapids, flowing over and around a thousand obstacles, the very agitation of those rapids oxygenating the water and making it vital to sustain life. There can be great and small adjustments of levels along the way, and from season to season, showing up as floods and waterfalls, the river adapting to its surroundings yet continuing on its path towards its destination.

Life is exactly like that, if we can just remember.

We get frustrated when our best laid plans take us on detours in life. We forget that detours are the very nature of life! There are no straight lines in nature, ever! See for yourself. I searched the web for a map of the Colorado river basin. The map of the Colorado, and its tributaries, looks like a train wreck! Rivers and streams and mountains and wanderings all over the place! No obvious rhyme or reason, no apparent order, and no straight lines. Not one. Yet look at the amazing beauty and power and life of that river and everything that it touches. Look at what it and its tributaries have created as they wander towards their destination.

If you can't see the perfection of God in a river, you're not looking closely enough. Every single piece, every single moment, every single twist and turn of the river is what makes it what it is. In its wandering, it is perfect. Life is exactly the same way.

By contrast, I flew into the Los Angeles airport recently, and had the opportunity to observe the Los Angeles River from the air. Yes, there is a river in L.A., such as it is. "We" decided at some point that we could manage that particular river better than God. It needed managing! It was unpredictable, uncontrollable! It wandered all over the place, flooded in winter, dried up in the summer. Surely we could do a better job managing that river than God. And so man invented concrete. And we paved the Los Angeles river. And now the river is, for all intents and purposes, dead. It is no longer a river as we know river. It is, to put it bluntly, more like a sewer. In our desire to take out all of the twists and turns, to remove the unpredictable nature of it, to smooth out all of the ups and downs so that we will know exactly what to expect at all times, we have killed it. If you ever long to experience straight lines in your life, to level out all of the bumps and waves and curves and experience instead a flat-line life experience, take a trip to the Los Angeles river first. Straight lines are not nearly as desirable as they may appear.

Life, like the river, is designed to wander. All that we judge and label as good and bad, right and wrong all has its perfect place within the whole of our lives. All of the unpredictability, the diversity, the various forms and experiences that life takes make life what it is, what it is supposed to be - a rich tapestry of as many different terrains and experiences as we can cram into one lifetime. Every "dead end" that you have ever experienced, every time that your life has doubled back on itself and it looks like you are going backwards instead of forward (called an "oxbow" in a river, which creates a lovely micro-environment all its own), every single rapid and waterfall and eddy and beaver-dam has its place.

The river knows how to be a river, just like Life knows how to do life. Both are designed to wander, and they wander well, if allowed to do so. We should all wander as well as a river.

Our ego, however, thinks it knows better. We spend a lifetime accumulating evidence, information, and data. We establish positions, opinions and perspectives about how things *should* be. We buy into agreements, largely unconsciously, like the one that says that the optimal way to get from point A in our lives to point B is the shortest distance - a straight line. Once we have bought in to that or any agreement, anything that shows up unlike it is immediately labeled bad or wrong, and we set out to fix it. We invest enormous amounts of time and energy trying to fix things that are not broken in the first place, and don't need to be fixed. We forget the nature of things.

This is not to say that there are not dramatic times in life that can get our attention, even stop us in our tracks. There are. A young person in our lives wanders 'off-track' and investigates an alternative path. Someone we know and love dies. A relationship goes sideways. When those things happen, what do we typically do? We freak out. We categorize these things as bad or wrong. Our life path, or that of someone we know, has taken an unexpected turn, and we don't like it. We think we know a better route, so we haul out our concrete and try to straighten and manage something that is just doing what is its nature to do; wander.

I got a note from a friend recently, about a conversation that she had with another mutual friend of ours.

Hi Jeff –

Jeff, I don't understand people. I love them, but I don't always understand them, and could use some advice. How do you deal with people who tell you that you HAVE to do something, that you HAVE to read this book or that, each time telling me that THIS has all the answers that I need! ANY suggestions would be welcome. Love you lots!

Phyl

Dear Phyl~

Here's what I see;

1) People are people, are going to do what they do and be what they are. We have no control over them. The sooner we concede that, the better.

2) The only thing that we have even a minimal amount of choice about is how we navigate the village, and the people in it. We do have that power, that choice, and no one, no matter what, can take that away from us.

3) We give that power away on a regular basis - the power of how we are going to feel at any given moment. This giving away of power is also a choice.

I have watched you and (our unnamed friend – who is really quite an amazing, conscious and loving guy) go round and round periodically for years. He dangles the bait, you bite, and the race is on. Notice the three parts of that scenario.

You have no control over the first – the bait. He is who he is. Everybody is who they are, and we get to let them be. People are going to be attached to their positions.

You have all of the power and choice over the second – your reaction. I myself am choosing more and more to simply not engage. It's like tai chi in consciousness. One cannot fight with me if I provide nothing to fight against. Not that we can't acknowledge and even honor the other persons position - even and perhaps especially when it challenges us, for it is in our challenges that we have an opportunity to stop, do a quick self-check inventory, and see if there is anything within us that needs to be realigned. Once we have done that, the final piece is letting it go, coming down the backside of the lovely wave that is built into anything and everything, rather than pitching a tent at its apex and extending an experience beyond its expiration date.

Your choice around the first and second aspects determines the third – whether the race takes place or not.

Love,

Jeff

In this example my friend Phyllis decided that something went wrong. A conversation (relationship) took an unexpected turn, and she didn't like it. From another perspective I saw an opportunity for her to reconsider how she navigated what happened. There is always another perspective.

Another of my teachers says, "It's not about what it appears to be about." In this case, it wasn't about what was contained within the conversation, but rather was about how she chose to navigate that conversation. Sometimes I can remember that, and sometimes I cannot, but the more I practice asking myself, "what is this really about?", the better I get at navigation.

When the river of life takes an unexpected turn, and someone else is involved, rather than looking at our part, our choices, our perspective, we want to make it about them. Sometimes we really, really want whatever it is that is causing us to struggle and suffer to be about them. We want to blame them for how we are feeling. But the minute we do that, we have given our power away. We have made our choice, handed our feelings and responses to "them" on a silver platter, and are, as a result of that choice, allowing them to determine how we feel.

I can always find a "them" to point to if I look hard enough. And I have absolutely no control over "them" nor they over me, not over what I think or feel or how I choose to navigate. They are not mine to fix. My work is always my work. What is mine to consider in a given situation? What is mine to choose? That is all that I have any real control over.

Viktor Frankl, survivor of the death camps of World War Two, is quoted as saying, "The one thing you can't take away from me is the way I choose to respond to what you do to me. The last of one's freedoms is to choose one's attitude in any given circumstance."

If he can do it under those most extreme of circumstances, surely we can do the same in ours.

To retain our choice, we must remain awake to the Truth that we have choice. We run into trouble when we forget that, when we are asleep. We wander out of the moment, into the past or into the future. We make up stories about what might happen. We even make up stories about what DID happen! We make it about them. We must be constantly mindful and present if we are to wander this life journey with the grace and peace that we desire to experience.

And how do we stay awake? Simple; we choose to, and, we practice. What if you were to start each and every day with a simple affirmation, reinforcing your choice to be awake and present and mindful today? What if you were to make that one commitment to your own heart and soul? How might that change your experience of life? Something as simple as, "Today I say YES to life" can be amazingly powerful. I have suggested this simple affirmation many times to many people, and have seen lives transformed as a result. Affirmations keep us mindful and aware. They shift our focus away from what we don't want to experience towards what we do want to experience.

Perhaps you choose something more specific, like, "I choose to be present and mindful as I wander today with grace and ease."

"Today I choose to be a place where love, kindness and compassion are expressed and experienced."

"Today I choose to wander well, trusting that the nature of Life supports and nourishes Itself, through and as me, in every moment."

"Today I trust the Spirit of Life that knows how to do what It does, as me, and as everyone that I meet."

Make up your own affirmation. Find the words and the feelings that work for you. Keep it short and simple. Print your affirmation(s) on 3 X 5 cards, and put one on your bathroom mirror, one in your car, one by your computer, one by your phone, one in your bag or pocket. Choose to practice mindful wandering. Your experience of life will immediately begin to change.

When we make this kind of choice, it may not be smooth sailing from here on out. We may not become instantly graceful. Within each of us are old beliefs and positions and fears that, though unhealthy, have become very well established in our consciousness. They have been running our lives for a long time. Those beliefs may not allow themselves to be displaced by these new choices of ours without some struggle. It is not uncommon for people to sabotage themselves, recreating situations and circumstances that are fueled by old beliefs, undermining the new belief system. The ego doesn't like to surrender its positions. It doesn't like to admit that it might have been wrong for all these years, that there might be a different way of looking at things, a gentler way of navigating life. Old beliefs might take some time to displace. It takes practice to wake up and begin to remember that we have choice, especially when we have not practiced choosing for years, or maybe ever.

One of my teachers went so far as to say that things might even get worse before they get better. She likened it to a beaker of water in which sediment has been allowed to settle to the bottom and remain there, undisturbed. It's mucky, and taints the water, but we get used to it and settle for it. When we begin to pour fresh, new water – new beliefs and choices, a new perspective on life - into that beaker, it is going to stir up the sediment. Things can get murky for a while as that sediment, by necessity, begins to be flushed from the beaker. If we stop pouring in clean water because things are stirred up, the sediment will eventually settle back where it was, continue to taint the water, and get stirred up whenever anything new is introduced.

Our thoughts and beliefs and positions are just like that.

The invitation is to continue pouring the clean, fresh water into the beaker regardless of the sediment that gets stirred up. We can do this consciously, knowing what we are doing, and why. It may get murky for a while. We may even get disoriented. Yet if we continue, no matter what, in time true clarity begins to happen.

"Yes I am consciously and intentionally choosing to stir up my own stuff, not because I am some kind of masochist, but to flush out any accumulated impurities that no longer serve me.

"Yes, I am doing this on purpose, with purpose – to change my thinking, to clear the water of my mind and heart and soul. Today I choose mindful wandering. I choose to consciously and intentionally reconsider every belief, every position, every fear, every pre-judgment and every limiting or self-deprecating thought. If those thoughts no longer serve me, I choose to let them go, as many times as it takes. Today I choose to be awake and aware. Today I choose to step into a bigger experience of life than my old beliefs and positions and fears have allowed me to do. Today, I step fully and completely into the river of life. And I say YES to the length and depth and richness and sweetness of it."

THE VILLAGE
AND THE
MOUNTAINTOP

"At some point in the journey, we may become tired, weary and confused. Homesick. All the mountains, the scenery, the food, the people, the experiences just don't do it for us anymore. We want to go home. What am I doing here, we wonder. Nothing worthwhile is happening. Yet, another part of us knows the truth and whispers, "Yes, something is happening, something worthwhile.""

~ Melody Beattie

Once upon a time there was a village. That village was home. It was sanctuary. It supported most all of our needs, and from it we learned most of what we needed to navigate our life path. In the village were our parents, aunts and uncles and cousins and children and wise elders. There was love and commonality and understanding. There was security, and safety, and there was comfort.

From infants to elders, the village contained and sustained all. There was a lovely symmetry in this, an interaction and interdependence that was mutually beneficial. The young learned from the old, and the old experienced joy in the young. There was organic, effortlessly sharing, a giving and receiving not just of resources but of energy and wisdom and love and of life itself.

A short distance from the village one could find a mountaintop, a hilltop, a field or a forest where they could experience isolation, time and space to commune with nature, to reflect, to meditate, to pray. When that need was met, one could return to the village, renewed and refilled, balance restored, and carry on participating in the vitality of life. There was perfect balance between community and self.

Sure, some would leave the village. Young people are called to explore, to go beyond what they have known. That, too, was and is the nature of things. But the village was the hub, the primary point of reference, and even those who left it took something of the village with them.

This has been the way of things, in one form or another, since we first stood upright. That is, until modern times. The industrial age made us mobile, and we were on the move. Villages spread and diversified, and got larger and busier. Families spread out, the young going further afield, often leaving the old behind. The fragmentation of the village began in earnest. Historically, this dissolution of the village is a very recent occurrence. In the blink of an eye, a mere blip on the human timeline, our whole social structure dramatically changed. Yet our needs – the inherent, hard-wired nature of human as social animal – did not change. As a result, there simply has not been time for us to adapt well.

We find ourselves living in a social model that is foreign to us; one of suburbs and cities where we don't know the names of the people living next door to us, let alone being mutually supportive in any real way. Families are no longer nuclear, but rather are spead across vast distances. The only real commonality of villages is geography.

Because we still have within us all of the needs that the historical village provided to us, we are developing new coping mechanisms to address those needs. And, like the development of any new tool, we are going about it rather clumsily. We haven't yet figured out how to recreate the organic, built-in way that the village, our primary point of reference, kept us balanced. We are largely out of balance, our basic needs unmet, resulting in major individual and societal dysfunction. Addiction, crime, feelings of isolation and separation, mental health issues, and even physical disease are the result.

This rather clumsy new model doesn't have the balance that the village gave us, but rather is showing up in a more polarized way. People are leaning heavily towards community, or running for the hills towards solitude. These days, there are village people, and there are mountaintop people.

Village people think mountaintop people are odd. Reclusive, quiet, inclined towards introversion, mountaintop people tend to sit back, watch, and consider things. They are happy listening to the wind in the trees, water flowing in a stream, or the silence of night. On the mountaintop there is time and space to consider not just what is all around us, but what is within. There is quiet enough to listen for the still, small voice of heart and soul. There is time for being, as well as doing.

Conversely, mountaintop people think village people are nuts. Generally more extroverted, village people are more urban oriented, and do well in towns and cities. They thrive on the hustle and bustle, are more impulsive, better in crowds. They are happiest when they are going, doing, on the move.

Not many people are all one way or the other. Whether we are aware of it or not, we all have the same needs and desires, in varying degrees, somewhere within us. The perfect balance is what we seek. Most of us fall somewhere in between being entirely mountaintop people or entirely village people. We all have aspects of both in us, and the sooner we become aware of our inclination, where the scales currently stand in our hearts and souls, the more comfortably we can navigate our daily life. We live within a society where both aspects – the village and the mountaintop – present themselves for us to choose from. We get to decide, more or less, how much of our time and energy we invest in the village experience, and how much we invest in the mountaintop experience. Therein lies the challenge.

Part of us craves the solitude, the peace, the symmetry and beauty and organic nature of nature itself, of the mountaintop. We need to recognize and honor that inner desire to have a place of relative quiet, where we can hear the breeze in the trees, and listen for that still, small voice within. But the fact is that the grocery store, the gas station, the experience of interpersonal relations – interacting and loving and witnessing each other, the community that we also want, need and desire to be a part of - are all to be found in the village.

It is also important to recognize that our wants and needs are not fixed in position. The scales of need and want within us may currently stand in one position and tomorrow, next year or 10 years from now that position may change. It's not a stable thing, our inclination. The opportunity here is to keep a finger on our own pulse, so to speak, to feel the subtle or perhaps not so subtle leanings that our heart and soul are communicating to us, in order that their needs be heard, honored, and met.

I was born and raised in Los Angeles, and thought that city life was normal. I thought that the city was the nature of things. I did fine there when I was young. I had no other points of reference, so while somewhere in my heart and soul I knew at some level, even then, that my natural leaning was not towards being a city boy, I had no real contrast, nothing to compare my current environment to. I didn't know what I was missing.

Then somewhere along the way I spent a summer with my grandparents on their farm in Indiana. In the course of one day I went from a lifelong reference point of Los Angeles living to a teeny tiny little town in rural Indiana named Andrews, whose population was less than 100 souls, most of whom were scattered far and wide on corn, wheat and soybean farms. I quickly learned the meaning of the word culture-shock.

Indiana is the flattest place on Earth. I'm sure that some atlas somewhere has statistical proof of this. It is actually dark at night. There are stars in Indiana that do not exist in Los Angeles. Indiana is also quiet. Not silent, but quiet. There are sounds and smells there that are not man-made. There is space where there are no buildings, no asphalt, nothing but dirt and grass and bugs. There are woods, and lanes, farm-ponds, and the muddy but mighty Wabash River. There are barnyards and chicken coops and fireflies. Indiana is magical.

After I recovered my senses, more or less, and got past literally being physically sick from being so disoriented, I began to explore. Though not exactly a mountaintop, Indiana was the closest thing to it that I had experienced in any real way. Oh, I had been to real mountaintops before. Big Bear and Lake Arrowhead are Los Angeles's version of the mountaintop. But since it they are so close to L.A., and since L.A. people must have all of the comforts of home strapped to their roof-racks, that area of the San Bernardino Mountains is, well, a suburban mountaintop. When you take all of the energy of the village to the mountaintop, eventually it just becomes a village with a higher elevation. Traffic and tract-homes and smog do not, in my mind, a mountaintop make.

As I was writing this chapter a friend of mine called and asked, "Where are my people? Where are the people that I can be myself with, where I can be comfortable and authentic without fear, where I can hang out and have real conversations?"

"Funny, I was just thinking about that," I replied.

"Well," she said, "I'm not sure where I am going to end up this summer. I may keep working here in Marin County, but I may hole-up in a cabin somewhere."

Check. I get it. This is exactly what is making the mountaintop more and more attractive for so many people. We can't find our people. We are malnourished due to lack of solitude and quiet. For those who are inclined, even slightly, towards the quiet side, city life can be a pressure cooker quite capable of driving one completely mad. I've seen it. OK, I admit it. I've felt it too. Unfortunately, since mountaintops are at a premium, we're creating them elsewhere - in our own homes and apartments, in our own minds and hearts. We're isolating, because the village has become, for many, unsafe. The energy in the village can be an assault on the senses. But we're stuck there. That's where the work is, where the resources are. So we withdraw, mentally, energetically, emotionally, even spiritually and become isolated, right smack in the middle of the village.

This creates conflict within us, for we are essentially social creatures. Interaction is critical to our well-being. Sanctuary is likewise critical to our well-being. How then do we find our way? How do we navigate this ever changing, ever moving line between a desire to be in sanctuary, to have a place where we can be safe and real and peaceful, and our need to interact, to be stimulated, to witness and participate in the vitality of village life? First we must become aware that this dynamic exists in our culture, and in our hearts and souls. Without the awareness, it's too easy to assume that we're nuts, that there is something inherently wrong with us. This then feeds into and reinforces the very sense of separation that we are seeking to heal in the first place.

There is nothing wrong with us. Let's get that on the table right now. There is nothing wrong with us. Everyone is wired a little differently, has different needs, and navigates this balance between village and mountaintop a little differently. That is as it has always been. We are unique individuals, yet we have also entered into another rather odd, largely unconscious agreement that we are supposed to be like everyone else. We're not. Get used to it. Then go beyond just getting used to it, and get comfortable with it. The invitation is for us to get to know ourselves, to become aware of, familiar with, and then comfortable with our needs, and our inclinations, and then learn to navigate accordingly.

When I don't get enough nature time, when it's too busy in the house for too long, when there is too much noise or too much running around, I get cranky, and I know exactly why. I need some mountaintop time.

I have a good friend who lives out in the country. Not too far, just far enough for her liking. It suits her. Before she retired, she used to drive in to town, which is really a fair-sized city in northern California. Most days she would make the drive to work, to attend church, to do whatever she needed to do, and then drive the 20 or so miles back out to her place in the country that is her sanctuary, her mountaintop. It took her some time and some work, but she figured out and now knows her village / mountaintop balance point pretty well. When she gets her fill of the village, she has no compunction about saying, "Had enough, gotta go!"

We don't all have that luxury of a place in the country. Some people wouldn't want it if they could.

I have another friend who is all city oriented. I asked her recently if she might be interested in joining a group of us to go white-water rafting.

"I don't do dirt." She told me. "I need clean sheets, cable, a taxi when I need it, and Starbucks. If they have that, I'll think about it." She is SO City.

Where to you fall on the village / mountaintop scale? And, more importantly, are you meeting your own needs?

I work with a lot of people, and the majority of them are out of balance in this area. Generally speaking we as a culture are way over-stimulated, and have forgotten what sanctuary looks and feels like. We live in a wound-up state from the moment we wake up until we collapse into bed at the end of the day. Run, run, run, faster, more, these are the unspoken agreements that we have made. This agreement is taking its toll on our bodies, our minds, our hearts and our souls. It's taking its toll on our relationships, on our self-image, and on our worldview. It is, as a whole, way out of balance.

I can't count the number of times that I have assigned, as homework to a client, a half day at the beach or the river, or a daytrip to an amazing grove of redwoods that we have nearby. They come back transformed. I had one person actually ask me, about the redwoods, "How long has that place been there?"

Oh, about three thousand years, give or take. It's 12 miles from where she lives.

It also helps to seek out and find, or to create, villages where you can find some degree of comfort and safety and commonality. This is happening more and more often in our society. Since the dissolution of the old village, we are creating new ones, villages that are safe, where there is commonality, comfort, and the opportunity to give and receive love in all of the ways that love shows up. I'm not speaking of actual villages where one lives full time, though there are those too; communal living situations. What I am referring to are the places that we can go and meet some of our village needs. They may not be like the villages of old, where most or all of our needs could be met in one place. We may need to participate in multiple villages in order to experience the balance that we seek. It may not be perfect, but it's a start. In northern California there are art and collective farming "villages", and there is a renewed interest and movement toward spiritual villages. Ecologically oriented villages, and now even virtual villages like Facebook and MySpace are meeting some of these needs.

I have a friend and colleague who facilitates vision quests. She takes people out into the mountains or the desert where they spend time alone with nature, with the silence, with themselves. Can you remember the last time you did anything like that? Have you ever?

The bottom line is that we all have our needs, in varying degrees. Figure out what your needs are, and decide, consciously and intentionally, to address them. When you do that, balance will begin to restore itself within your being. Find a mountaintop, whatever your mountaintop may be, and go and sit there for a while. Notice what you feel. If you can, sit there long enough for your mind and heart and soul to get quiet, especially if you are a village person, always on the go, never seeming to have enough time in the day. Reacquaint yourself with a mountaintop. Doing so may allow you to navigate the village, and the village people, in a more balanced and healthy way than ever before.

HOLD IT LIGHTLY

"Look deep into nature, and then you will understand everything better."

~ Albert Einstein

In an earlier chapter I spoke of an old teacher of mine who often said, "Attachment is the cause of all of your suffering."

I was attached so tightly to so many things – people, ideas, positions, beliefs and fears - that I often left claw-marks on things when any movement at all began to happen. There were times when it felt, figuratively speaking, like my fingernails were ripping right out of their beds because I was holding on so tight. I left a wide swath of claw-marks in my wake. And, I suffered.

It is the nature of life, the nature of all form, to constantly shift and move. Life is not static or fixed. Like the river, it is always flowing. Change is the only real constant. When I align myself with that nature, navigation becomes a very different experience than it used to be.

It is not my job to hold things in place. It is not my job to make sure that things remain the same. It is not my job to resist every shift and movement and realignment that comes my way. It is not my job to hold onto a belief because of an underlying fear of change. If I choose to do that, then I am causing my own suffering. I cannot blame it on you, or them, or it. I must take responsibility.

I was in meditation one day, struggling and suffering, when a couple of images came to mind. The first was of a fine bowl, shallow and delicate and translucent, not regular around the edges but with dips and curves. It fit comfortably in my hands, and I realized that this was a symbol of the container within which my thoughts and feelings and emotions can be held in any given moment. There were no high sides designed to contain anything. Indeed, the design seemed just the opposite of that. The design was not conducive to holding anything for long, but rather to be a place where ideas, feelings, and experiences can rest temporarily until they shift or are displaced by something new.

The image morphed into my own hands, or perhaps more accurately into a pair of fine hands, cupped together, shallow, open, receptive, yet not clingy or attached. I think of those hands often, and have invited many people along the way to consider the possibility of holding what they are struggling with in this manner, holding it very lightly, letting it move and shift and find whatever new alignment it is trying to find.

In the wave chapter, I spoke of waves of emotion, of feeling, of experience. Waves are not meant to be held or kept in place. It is their nature to be in constant motion.

All form is like that. People, places, experiences, jobs, even our bodies are all constantly changing, shifting, realigning. They are not, in the end, ours to hold but rather are ours to experience, as they are, while they are. And then they will change. Day to day, moment by moment, these things will change.

A decision to hold things lightly allows for things to come, to pass, to shift and move and evolve as they are designed to do. I have been practicing this choice now for many years. Sometimes I am completely successful with it. Sometimes, less so. It is a practice. We are human, after all, and are fabulously messy. We get beat up (and beat ourselves up). We stumble and fall. We break open and spill all over the place. We learn, grow, and expand. This is the nature of things. Growing pains at any age are not necessarily fun, but especially so for people of a certain age. Young people are much more flexible. They don't seem to need this constant reminder to hold things lightly. Their fingernails are not so rigid.

The longer that we live, however, the more attached we become to a certain way of looking at things, a worldview, expectations of how people should be, of what is right and what is wrong. Can we hold our beliefs lightly enough for them to move when they are inclined to do so, when it's time for them to shift or expand or even to fall away? We should ask ourselves that question often, because it is easy to forget.

My partner is vegan. She was raised in San Francisco, and is very open-minded when it comes to food. She introduced me to things like tofu (yuck!), spring rolls

(Thai food, yuck!), nut milk (yuck! I like REAL milk!), and the list goes on. I learned that I was very attached to some beliefs around food. And as a result, I suffered. And I made her suffer right along with me. Fair is fair.

I moaned and whined and picked and grimaced. I complained and threatened and stubbornly stood my ground. I was very attached to my beliefs. Milk does a body good, right? Well, as it turns out, maybe not so much. Little by little, I began to let my experience shift, to move and change. Before I knew what was happening, one of my new favorite dishes was pesto on spinach pasta (but it's all GREEN!) and salad (Holy mother my whole meal is green! Where's the beef!?).

I was not awake to the state of our food industry, nor did I particularly want to be. I was very attached to my beliefs, to the way that I was raised (meat and potatoes, and please pass the butter and gravy), to the indoctrinated virtues touted by the food industry. Honestly I am still very much in the process of adjusting my eating habits. People have quite an intimate day to day affair with food, and we are very attached to our beliefs about it.

I don't want to wander too far into food. That is a voluminous topic in and of itself, and honestly I don't know enough about it to speak to it with any real authority. It is however a great example of something that I had not consciously considered my attachment to.

Where else have we fallen asleep, acting and choosing and perceiving from a place of unconscious attachment? Dishes should be rinsed and put in the sink immediately after use. Children do their homework and chores before play. God is an old white guy with a beard in the sky who keeps track of transgressions and hurls random lightning bolts at unsuspecting humans. If the seat was meant to stay down, it wouldn't have hinges. The toothpaste tube is rolled from the bottom up, never squished midway.

What if we were to allow for the possibility that some of our beliefs may be – how do I say this gently – wrong? Could it be? Is it even remotely possible that there might be another position or opinion that is viable, perhaps even more in alignment with the nature of things than our own? Can I hold my own beliefs lightly enough to let them move when it is time for them to move, shift, realign, expand, or even fall away? That is what is before us to consider.

Consider what our dominant positions and beliefs and opinions have created thus far. Our planet is in sad shape and getting worse by the day. Wars are fought over religion and money, fear and separation. There is hate in our own communities, in our own households, in our own minds. Clearly, something has got to give. We can wait all day for "them" to change, but as Gandhi invited us to consider, "Be the change you wish to see."

Someone has to be first. Someone has to step back from the ego position of attachment to being right and allow for movement. Someone has to step up and say, "OK, I'm willing to look again." If we wait for "them", and cannot learn to hold things lightly, we may have waited too long.

EVERYBODY DOES IT DIFFERENT

"The seven blind men who gave seven different descriptions of the elephant were all right from their respective points of view."

~ Mohandas K. Gandhi

This could be a four word chapter. If we really get this idea, and practice it, it can eliminate a huge portion of the angst that we experience on a daily basis.

Repeat after me: Everybody. Does. It. Different.

People get very attached to a certain way of doing things. Our way of doing things is THE right way, the best way, the only way. This belief is quickly followed by the one that says that if everyone just believed and acted as we do, the whole planet would be a much better place.

So, let me get this straight. You have learned, most likely from someone else, how something "should" be done. The house is cleaned in a certain way, dishes go in the dishwasher a certain way, the toothpaste tube, the toilet paper roll, laundry folding, meeting conducting,

God worshipping, whatever the belief is about. Your way is the right way and anything else is the wrong way. There is only one right possibility, and a million wrong ones.

Can you see how this way of thinking might seriously impede our ability to be open, accepting, receptive, and happy? There are a billion or so other people on this planet with a few billion different ways of doing things, and if we cannot open to the possibility that there may be more than one right way to go about living life, we will suffer, and suffer greatly, guaranteed. "They" are not all wrong. This is also guaranteed.

In school we were taught that there is one right answer and if you don't have the right answer, you have the wrong answer. This became ingrained in us, and in our group mind. We all tacitly agreed to this model and it became the rule; There Is Only One Right Answer. But what if the model itself is flawed? What if there are many right answers? Even more audacious to consider, what if there is no wrong answer? What if it really is ok if the toilet paper roll goes under instead of over the top? What if there are many paths to a greater experience of God? Can we expand our consciousness and loosen our attachment to the need to have THE right answer long enough to consider that, in this universe of infinite possibility, there may be many right answers?

In the introduction to this book I mentioned my visit to a Buddhist temple when I was young. The realization that I had upon experiencing that temple and wandering the grounds was that this was a holy place, a place of deep roots and commitment to a way of life that was no less sacred than the protestant churches of my youth. I thought that day of what I had been taught, that there was only one way to God, and I knew then that the model was flawed. The Buddhist monks were every bit as holy as the ministers and congregants of the Christian churches that were my early cultural points of reference. To this day it feels a little blasphemous even to consider such a thing, but Jesus taught of love and non-judgment and inclusivity. He didn't exclude anyone. I think he would have enjoyed those monks immensely.

Years later I had a world religions teacher who told me something else that changed my thinking permanently. "Give me a topic or an issue," he said, "and choose a position, for or against, and I will find you at least half a dozen statements in the Bible to reinforce that position."

We love to be right, and have become experts at collecting evidence to reinforce our position. But the fact is, especially now that we have access to global resources at our fingertips, there is a wealth of evidence for or against many, most, or even of all positions. Even when there is overwhelming evidence of something, global warming for example, you can easily collect evidence and build a case that it is not really happening.

A classic example to illustrate the point is that of ten people who witness a traffic accident. Though they witness exactly the same event, they experience those moments in ten very different ways. They see and experience the event not objectively, but subjectively. They experience not what happened, but their perception of what happened, based on the beliefs, positions and prejudices accumulated over their lifetime. Those accumulated beliefs and positions are the lenses through which we see our world. We overlay our positions on to what happens, and reach conclusions based not on what happened, but rather based on what we believe about what happened.

Continuing with this illustration, lets say the accident involves a young mother and an elderly person, both driving. An elderly person witnessing the event identifies with the elderly person in the accident. They see someone like themselves, someone that they can relate to. They themselves are careful and responsible so might assume that the elderly driver a responsible, careful driver. This prejudices their view of events. A young mother witnesses the same event and sympathizes with the other driver. She assumes that, like her, the young drivers' top priority is the safety and welfare of her children, that she is super-responsible, and probably the better driver of the two. This prejudices her view of events. This isn't about right or wrong. It's about perception, and interpretation. This is how our minds work.

The invitation here is to hold right and wrong very lightly, to soften the hardness that often occurs when we take a position on something and become convinced that we have THE right answer. Become aware of the evidence that you are collecting and of your motives as you collect it. You will then be aware of your own process, your own perception and interpretation of things. Awareness gives us a better understanding of what our own positions are, why they are, and where they came from, which in turn allows us to understand other people and their positions more expansively.

I did a web-search on "toilet paper roll, which way is the right way". On a subject this simple, with only two possible primary options, I got three million, ten thousand hits. There are three million, ten thousand posts and discussions currently available on the web with a position about which is the right way to hang toilet paper. I searched the phrase, "which is the right religion?". Sixty seven million hits. Out of those sixty seven million positions is there one, definitive, absolutely positively right answer? If so, that would mean that there are roughly sixty six million, nine hundred ninety nine thousand, nine hundred and ninety nine wrong answers.

Even within a given religion, political party or belief system of any kind, every single person is going to have a unique experience. If you are involved with a community of any kind you might ask yourself, does everyone in the group agree with everything all of the time? If you're honest with yourself, the answer is no, they don't. Each person brings a little something different to the table for consideration. This is as it should be. This is the Divine design of unique individuality. Everybody does it different. If there was no diversity of position, there would be no choice, and no free will. We would all be vanilla cookie cutter people, doing and thinking and acting the same way. We would all wear the same clothes, drive the same cars, eat the exact same foods, and live happily every after, right? Actually I think we would be bored out of our skulls and go crazy in very short order. Sameness is simply not the nature of things. Diversity is.

The nature of creation is that no two things are exactly alike. Something as simple as snowflakes reminds us of this infinite diversity. Scientists tell us that in the history of the planet there have never been two snowflakes exactly the same. Likewise, each and every human being on this planet is going to have a unique, individual worldview, talent, perspective, and contribution. This is as it should be. This is the design, the nature of things. We are not supposed to be all the same and agree on everything all of the time. Once we realize this, the invitation and the opportunity is to align the way that we navigate thought this infinite maze of personal interaction on a daily basis with the designed diversity, rather than to resist and struggle against it. As each snowflake is unique, so is each individual. Snowflakes seem to get along just fine.

Everybody does it different. The sooner we get used to the idea of diversity, accept it, appreciate the nature of it and align ourselves with it, the sooner we will stop struggling against and suffering because of a Divine design that is inherent in all of creation.

THE EYES OF GOD

"Everything that exists has brought with it its own peculiar lesson. The mountain teaches stability and grandeur; the ocean, immensity and change. Forests, lakes, and rivers, clouds and winds, stars and flowers, stupendous glaciers and crystal snowflakes - every form of animate or inanimate existence, leaves its impress upon the soul of man."

~ Orison Swett Marden

It can be almost effortless to see and to sense the divinity, the beauty and the perfection in nature. It is such an amazing orchestration of life, time, matter and the great intangible; consciousness. One can almost sense, within it all, a Presence, a wisdom, and a love. That's why we return to nature again and again. It seems to be the easiest place to remember, beyond and beneath thought or fact or data, the symmetry of Creator and creation.

I must return to the mountaintop, which in my case may be a mountaintop, or a lake, or a field or meadow or forest, or, most likely, a river, again and again. It calms my heart, and it feeds my soul. It allows me to practice the knowing that I desire to experience and to be rooted in, regardless of where I find myself. I want to see and experience all of life the way that I see and experience nature. Whether I am on the mountaintop or in the village, I want to see it all as Divine and perfect. That is my true desire. Surely that is how God sees Its creation.

I've gotten pretty good at this practice. It is relatively easy for me to see and to know your perfection and beauty, to experience your light, and sense the inherent divinity and goodness of your heart and soul. This, despite the fact that you – people in general – can be very challenging, as can my judgments and opinions of you. It is an ongoing process of letting go of those positions that don't support my true desire. In nature, I get it. With you, I continue to practice and learn to get it.

I have a much harder time seeing myself in the same way. It took me a while to figure out why. Why do we judge ourselves so harshly? Why do we find it so much easier to dwell on what we are not, what we "lack", rather than on what is good and right? The answer came to me in a meditation some years ago.

With nature, all is in the moment. I am present in nature. I don't concern myself with past or future. Because nature is nature, I have no inherent conflict with it. I can't have a personality issue with it. I may create a fleeting difference of opinion with it occasionally, but that is a futile and silly position to adopt, let alone try to be right about, so I release it almost as soon as it appears. I see nature essentially without judgment, as an observer. My experience of nature is relatively objective.

You – and by you I mean any you, people in general - fall somewhere between nature and me on the challenge scale. It is a little more difficult to see the divinity in you than it is to see it in the river. You are more similar to me, therefore have a greater capacity to reflect back to me aspects of myself that I might not care for.

But even given that, what I realized in my meditation that day is that I still see you in a much clearer way than I see myself. I don't know all of your history, your wounds, and your prejudices. I don't know all of the things that you have done, the places that you have been, the shame and insecurity and fear that has lived in you, and may still. I don't know all of the things that you judge yourself by and limit yourself with. I see you as you are in the moment, unimpeded and unencumbered by the past. I see you as a child of God, a deliberate, intentional, unique and individual expression of Divine Mind and Heart. I see you as a place for God to express and to experience life, a place for the good of God to show up in the world through and as you. You do it differently than I do, but that is at it should be, and does not prevent me from recognizing your inherent Divinity. I look at you from an angle that allows me to see around anything that you have collected in your mind and heart and soul. Your collection of evidence doesn't interest me, nor does it interest God.

The only time that I have trouble with this is when I decide that I need to make up a story about you, most often based on a snapshot, and most often having no basis in actual fact. We do that a lot. We love our snapshots. We take a snapshot of someone in any given moment or situation, and we extrapolate from there. We make a snap-judgment, and create a story about that person. This is something that I am constantly vigilant about. The snapshots that we experience of people are extremely limited, and limiting. We have no idea what that person has been through, what they are thinking and feeling, what challenges they may be facing. So, lacking facts, we make things up.

Grocery stores may be the most fascinating places on the planet to observe people, and to observe ourselves with people. I was going to the grocery store recently and was looking for a place to park, when I noticed a brand-new SUV whip into the parking lot, make a bee-line for the handicapped parking spot closest to the front door, slide right into that spot and park. I took a snapshot, and the story in my head began.

"Wow, nice SUV. I'd like one like that. But what a jerk, driving too fast in a parking lot, taking a space it sure doesn't look like they need." I needed evidence. I parked, watching, planning my route into the store to take me in for closer look at the SUV and its driver. Apparently I had nothing better to do.

Out of the vehicle hops this 30-something woman, apparently as healthy as me, and she proceeds to hustle herself right on into the store like nobody's business.

"I hate it when people park in handicapped spaces," I told myself. "somebody might REALLY need it." But then I saw that there was a handicapped placard hanging from the rearview mirror. "I'll bet it's not even her car. Maybe the placard isn't hers. Maybe she took it out of her mom's car. Yep, her Mom probably had to co-sign for that SUV too. Nice SUV." I headed into the store to collect more evidence. And then I realized what I was doing. I had taken a snapshot, and was creating a story based on nothing more than a woman parking at the grocery store. You can see how this gets in the way of seeing the divinity of people.

When I look at myself, I do have evidence. My story is not a guess, but is based on my experience. For many years I saw myself through a lifetime of accumulated grime, through a lens that has been splattered and pitted with a lifetime of unchallenged accumulated beliefs. Every hurt, every doubt, every fear and regret that I experienced along the way added another layer of grit to the lens through which I saw myself until it became impossible see myself clearly. My history files, my evidence, my accumulated grime all severely distorted my perception of myself. It can take some time to clean that mess up.

From Dr. Ernest Holmes I learned one of the most liberating concepts that I have ever heard. It's not a new idea. I have heard it before, presented in different ways, but sometimes we hear something presented in just the right way and at just the right time. Something clicks into place, and understanding happens. The concept is, "Principle is not bound by precedent."

When he speaks of Principle (with a capitol "P"), he is speaking to the presence, the possibility, the power, the love and the grace of God. He calls it by various names; Creative Life Principle, Eternal Principle, the Principle of Being, Divine Presence, the Source, Divine Givingness, First Cause, The Principle of Unity. "God, the Divine or Universal Life Principle, or whatever we choose to call It." Principle, or God, is not bound by precedent. It doesn't matter what has come before this moment. The Allness of God is not bound by anything in our history files. It cannot be limited or impeded by precedent, or by anything that happened before this moment. Evidence is rendered moot. Each moment we are born again, immersed in all of the possibility that we started this lifetime with.

Since all of creation, including you and I, exist within the Allness of God, this statement – Principle is not bound by precedent - has huge implications. It doesn't matter who we have been, where we have been, or what we have been. Each moment is unbound, un-tethered to any previous moment. The Christian tradition would call this being washed clean. Many faith traditions speak to this, but it wasn't until years after I first read this statement by Dr. Holmes that its full implication hit me. We are as free as we allow ourselves to be, right now, in this moment. Principle is not bound by precedent!

This explains why I have the experience of nature that I do. I am present with nature. History files are rendered moot in the face of the perfection of the moment. What if I could learn to see myself in that way, in the same way that I seem to so easily see nature, and have learned to be able to see you? During the meditation that I mentioned earlier I was able to do just that. I was able to change the lens through which I looked at myself, to step off to the side and see myself free of the story, the wounds and the mistakes. I was able to see my essence, my Truth, my heart and my soul. I saw my innocence, and the purity that is still in there at the core of my being. It was as if I were looking at myself through the eyes of God.

What if I could see everything that way? What if I could wake up every day and see the world through the eyes of God, untainted by any accumulated grime? What might my world look like then? This is the level of awareness that I aspire to. And, it's not always easy. Life presents us with circumstances and situations every day that don't always look or feel good, or godly, or divine. We live in a world that moves fast and is rapidly changing. It can feel like a lot to navigate while still remaining in a place of seeing and knowing the perfect Divinity of all, all of the time. Seeing our world and our lives through the eyes of God seems especially challenging when not just our heads, but our hearts are involved. We're experts at collecting evidence, and we can collect it for whatever position we choose.

I found myself in a situation recently that resulted in my experiencing great heartache. My head knew that ultimately this was a good thing, that there would be realization, change, expansion and growth as a result. Mentally I recognized the spiritual nature of the experience very clearly. I recognized the opportunity that was presenting itself. This was a chance for me to review things, to let go of some beliefs, positions and constriction that no longer served me and to experience God in a greater way as a result of this awakening. Yet my heart ached. To the core of my being it ached. There were times when I laid in my bed in the dark night, trying to sleep, trying to draw up from within me the knowing of the Allness of God in an effort to displace the heartache, and it just wouldn't happen. Not in those moments.

I knew then that I was not supposed to escape, deny, or fix the ache, but rather that there was something right in the middle of it for me to realize. Somewhere in the broken-open place inside of me was God, waiting to meet me. It was an opportunity to see myself again, even in my pain, through those eyes that are not clouded by self-doubt or self-judgment, but instead see the heart and soul with startling clarity, and know a Truth that transcends circumstance or situation. That was not a fun realization, that somehow the pain was serving me, facilitating a greater realization of life and of love and of God and of myself. That wasn't the answer that I wanted. I wanted the pain to stop. But had it stopped, I would not have realized what I did as a result of experiencing it.

As a society we are very pain avoidant. At the first sign of any pain, we scramble and set about fixing it. What I am suggesting here is that pain, especially heart-ache, has always existed. And everything exists within God. Since it has always existed, within God, it must have a purpose.

I have seen time and time again huge shifts in minds and hearts happen when the heart is most open, sometimes broken open. There might be something available in that place of the broken open heart that is perhaps not accessible in common times. I knew, in this case, that there was something there, and that it was critical to my own evolution as a spiritual being to stay in it until I found out what it was. That experience may be another book altogether. Suffice it to say, what I found in my own broken-open heart was a love bigger and deeper and richer than I had previously known.

I know in my heart of hearts that God is all, in all, through all. Likewise I know that the nature of God is love, in its infinite iterations and incarnations. I know that God is always, regardless of situation or circumstance, seeking greater experience and expression of Itself through and as every person on this planet. I am no exception, nor are you. There are no exceptions. There is no escape from Allness. No one was left out when the essential nature of Love was given, regardless of any evidence to the contrary. Our challenge, always, is to see and to recognize that Truth, no matter how messy things may appear, no matter how painful the ache, no matter how deeply broken-open we may feel.

There are going to be challenges in life. In order for us to live in an awakened state, there must be constant change, growth, and expansion. The status quo lulls us to sleep, and we begin to miss things, to forget how amazing life is, within us and all around us. We forget how richly blessed we are, how much, even in the most challenging of times, we have to be grateful for. We forget that Love is the greatest power and that ultimately nothing can stand before it.

Change is the nature of God in form. While the essential nature of God is changeless, in form – as people, situations and circumstances – life is fluid, ever shifting and evolving. Life is like a river. That is as it should be. That is the nature of things. So we find ourselves in this amazing place of having a foot in both worlds. One foot stands in a timeless and unchanging Truth, while another is planted in the ever shifting, changing, expanding world of Life.

Since our rational, logical, linear minds interpret things one way, and our hearts and souls interpret things another, there is an inherent paradox that we must first recognize, and then learn how to navigate. Truth in one part of us will not always align flawlessly with the facts and data gathered by the other. Ultimately it is this struggle that I am called to surrender, again and again. I am willing to concede that life doesn't always make sense, and likewise to concede that my finite mind is perhaps not capable at this point in my journey of fully understanding an infinite God.

It is my quest to see the world, myself, and you, through the eyes of God in such a way that allows me a measure of peace when life appears less than peaceful. It is by applying the tools that I have outlined in these pages that I am able to move through what often feels like a chaotic and confusing world with a modicum of grace and an ever-deepening faith. It is my trust in the ultimate loving nature of God that I hold onto, when all else falls away.

CPSIA information can be obtained at www.ICGtesting.com
Printed in the USA
LVOW071952100512

281083LV00001B/1/P